Twayne's English Authors Series

EDITOR OF THIS VOLUME

Kinley Roby

Northeastern University

Harold Pinter

REVISED EDITION

TEAS 51

Harold Pinter

HAROLD PINTER

By ARNOLD P. HINCHLIFFE
University of Manchester (England)

REVISED EDITION

TWAYNE PUBLISHERS
A DIVISION OF G. K. HALL & CO., BOSTON

Copyright © 1981 by G. K. Hall & Co.

Published in 1981 by Twayne Publishers,
A Division of G. K. Hall & Co.
All Rights Reserved

Printed on permanent/durable acid-free paper and bound
in the United States of America

First Printing

Photograph of Harold Pinter by Sam Siegel

Library of Congress Cataloging in Publication Data

Hinchliffe, Arnold P   1930–
        Harold Pinter.

(Twayne's English authors series ; TEAS 51)
Bibliography: p. 169–75
Includes index.
1.   Pinter, Harold, 1930–   —Criticism and interpretation.
    PR6066.I53Z675 1981   822'.914   80-24903
            ISBN 0-8057-6784-3

To
My Mother

Contents

About the Author

Arnold P. Hinchliffe was born in 1930 at Dewsbury (Yorkshire) and educated at Ossett Grammar School. After serving two years in the Royal Engineers he went to Manchester University, where he took a First Class Honors Degree in English Literature. In 1955, he graduated from Manchester as M.A. and left for the United States. He spent a year as English Speaking Union Fellow at Yale and received an M.A. from the American Studies Department. Returning to teach in the Department of English at Manchester University, he completed his Ph.D. in 1963 on symbolism in the American novel. Since then he has turned his attention to British Drama. He is now a Senior Lecturer in English Literature at Manchester University. His other books include two volumes in "The Critical Idiom" series, *The Absurd* (which has been translated into Greek, Japanese, Korean, and Arabic) and *Modern Verse Drama*, a Casebook on T. S. Eliot's *The Waste Land* (coedited with C. B. Cox), a Casebook on drama criticism, *Drama Criticism: Developments Since Ibsen*, and a study of recent British Theatre, *British Theatre: 1950–70*. At present he is working on a study of T. S. Eliot's *Murder in the Cathedral*.

Preface

In the preface to *Experimental Drama*, a symposium published in 1963, W. A. Armstrong explained the vitality of contemporary British drama as the meeting between imagination and complacency:

Beckett's enigmatic Godot has sent a religious tremor through a predominantly secular age: Pinter's haunted heroes have been a salutary reminder of what we still have to face when the Welfare State has done its best (or worst) for us: the tirades of Osborne's Jimmy Porter and the snide patter of his Archie Rice have emboldened the young and goaded their elders: Behan's Quare Fellow looms insistently over the issue of capital punishment: Bolt's Sir Thomas More, O'Casey's Father Ned, and Wesker's Beatie Bryant have likewise spoken to the conscience through the medium of the play.

It used to be habitual to think of British theater as vital and promising, and starting in 1956; yet one or two of the names above already strike a note of quaintness. And when Bamber Gascoigne wrote a New Year's article for the *Observer* in 1964 he called it "Keeping Up with the Crisis" and reminded us that 1963 had not produced a single striking new play. In this he echoed Kenneth Tynan, who had suggested, in *Tynan on Theater* (reprinted 1963), that all was not well, and in the August 1964 issue of *Plays and Players* John Russell Taylor continued the theme in an article called "What's Happening to the New Dramatists?" Not much, apparently. But then, as Gascoigne pointed out, 1594 was also a bad year: Thomas Kyd was dead without living up to his promise; Christopher Marlowe had been killed in suspicious circumstances; and Robert Greene had died of overindulgence. Only Shakespeare was left, a dramatist who had shown signs of promise but then gone commercial by writing a huge star part for Richard Burbage in *Richard III*. In 1964, the quatercentenary year, it was encouraging to remember how black 1594 had seemed.

Of all the dramatists who emerged to create this sense of a vital theater Harold Pinter seemed, to me, the most interesting. I hope the following pages will suggest why. The critic has an obligation to dive in as soon as possible even if it means making mistakes. The so-called complexity of a Pinter play seems to be of a peculiar kind: it exists after the event when the audience leaves the auditorium and asks the fatal question: "But what does it mean?" Terence Rattigan's reported exchange with Pinter is an example of this very human if secondary response: "When I saw *The Caretaker* I told Pinter that I knew what it meant. 'It's about the God of the Old Testament, the God of the New, and Humanity, isn't it?' Pinter said blankly, 'No, Terry, it's about a caretaker and two brothers.'" Similarly, when directing *The Lover* Pinter is reported to have said: "We're not quite sure of the author's intention here." Neither of these reports rings untrue, nor, I am sure, are they simply examples of authorial mischievousness. In a radio interview with Laurence Kitchin, Pinter described his own commentary on the plays as a complete waste of time. He has to come to his own plays objectively, like anyone else:

> I don't want to sound a mystificator, if there's a word, but I really do not know what . . . is in the script from A to Z by any means. I think it would be an impertinence of me to say that I did. . . . As a director my function is really to look at the text quite independently and objectively really and truly and the only thing is I do of course . . . happen to have something of the certain inner word. I mean someone. I know a little more. I've got something out of the horse's mouth. I've got a hot tip you know. . . .

Pinter continues to insist that his plays are simple and straightforward and that he has nothing to say about them. And so they are until we ask what they mean; by which too many people mean allegory and symbol. This book is partly a history of that particular question and how it has been answered, partly a history of recent British drama as Pinter has contributed to it, and partly a history of his own development. It is also a history of the developing tolerance to his methods. In revising this work in 1979 it is clear that revision must take a form more radical than the addition of notes on plays since *The Homecoming*. It must also take note of the huge cairn of criticism that has piled up over twenty years. It still reflects, however, the recognition that Pinter continues to surprise, puzzle, tease, and delight. Indeed in many respects he is the only one of that so-called renaissance in the 1950s who does continue to do so. There has been very little recent work from Osborne or Wesker that matches their early plays; Arden is no longer in commercial theater or distinguishable from his wife, D'Arcy, and Beckett, according to the logic of his plays, has dwindled. But the variety and power of Pinter's work remains. It stems from his quintessential Englishness (I am tempted to say from his London-ness). We need no longer struggle to define him as an Absurd dramatist. His work fuses aspects of European theater with the English way of life and English manners; it is this fusion of the foreign and native, the timeless and the universal with the particular and local, that gives the plays their enduring quality. He will remain one of Britain's most important twentieth-century dramatists—in my opinion, the most important.

ARNOLD P. HINCHLIFFE

Manchester, England

Acknowledgments

I am deeply indebted to Harold Pinter, not merely for permission to use unpublished and broadcast material, but also for the interest he has shown in the work as it proceeded. I should also like to thank Joseph Losey and Warner Pathé for help in connection with *The Servant;* Iain Hamilton for sending me the first publication of "A Slight Ache"; Alan Hancox for assistance in tracking down Pinter's poetry; Peter Wait and Methuen for continued assistance with the published texts of Pinter; the staff of the British Museum Reading Room for research into the first publication of "The Examination," and John Kershaw of A.T.V. Ltd. for the script of the *Tempo* program in October 1965.

I should like to thank Zdzislaw Mikulski for his translation of the article by Gregorz Sinko and Professor Sinko for permission to use it; David L. Hirst and Andrew P. Debicki, who found texts and criticism for me, and, in this revised edition, I am particularly grateful to the editor, Kinley E. Roby, Mrs. M. Wayt, who typed it, and Jim, who endured the revising.

The following permissions to quote from and refer to published works are acknowledged:

From *Stratford-on-Avon Studies*, No. 4, edited by J. R. Brown and B. Harris, for chapters by Clifford Leech and R. D. Smith. Copyright © Edward Arnold (Publishers), Ltd.

From *Experimental Drama*, edited by W. A. Armstrong, for essays by W. A. Armstrong, Geoffrey Bullough, and Martin Esslin. Copyright © 1963 by G. Bell and Sons, Ltd.

From *Harold Pinter*, by John Russell Taylor, "Writers and Their Works," No. 212. Copyright © "The British Council."

From *The Dark Comedy*, by J. L. Styan. Copyright © 1962 by Cambridge University Press.

From *Snakes and Ladders*, by Dirk Bogarde. By permission of the author and Chatto and Windus Ltd.

From *The Theater of the Absurd*, by Martin Esslin. Copyright © by Martin Esslin. Reprinted by permission of Doubleday and Company, Inc.

Acknowledgments

From *butter's going up*, by Steven H. Gale. Copyright © 1977, Duke University Press.

From *The Birthday Party*, review by Irving Wardle in *Encore* (July–August) 1958, by permission of the editors.

From *Mid-Century Drama*, by Laurence Kitchin. Copyright © 1960 by Faber and Faber, Ltd.

From "Joseph Losey and The Servant," by Jacques Brunius in *Film* 38, by permission of the editor.

From "The Theatre of the Absurd—How Absurd?" by David Tutaev in *Gambit*, by permission of the editor.

From *The Plays of Harold Pinter*. Copyright © Harold Pinter. Reprinted by permission of Grove Press, Inc., and Eyre-Methuen, Ltd.

From *Anger and After*, by John Russell Taylor. Copyright © 1969 John Russell Taylor, reprinted by permission of Methuen and Co., Ltd.

From *Strindberg: Plays*, translated by Michael Meyer. Reprinted by permission of Methuen and Co., Ltd.

From *Pinter: A Study of His Plays*, by Martin Esslin. Reprinted by permission of Methuen and Co., Ltd.

From *Modern Drama*, for the articles by J. T. Boulton, "Harold Pinter: The Caretaker and Other Plays" (September 1963), and J. Hoefer, "Pinter and Whiting: Two Attitudes towards the Alienated Artist" (February 1962), by permission of the editor.

From *New Theater Magazine*, for the article by Harold Pinter, "Harold Pinter Replies" (January 1961), and the John Arden review of *The Caretaker* (July 1960), by permission of the editor.

From *The Theater of Protest and Paradox*, by G. E. Wellwarth. Copyright © 1964 by New York University Press.

From *Nausea*, by Jean-Paul Sartre, translated by Lloyd Alexander, by permission of the publishers, New Directions.

From *Harold Pinter* by William Baker and Stephen Ely Tabachnick, by permission of the authors.

From *Alain Resnais* by James Monaco, by permission of the author and Martin Secker and Warburg, Ltd.

From *New English Dramatists*, No. 3, by J. W. Lambert, by permission of Penguin Books Ltd.

From *Sexual Deviations* by Anthony Storr, by permission of Penguin Books Ltd.

From *The Pinter Problem*, by Austin E. Quigley. Copyright © 1975, Princeton University Press.

From *Tulane Drama Review*, for "The Theater of Harold Pinter" by Bernard Dukore (March 1962), by permission of the editor.

From *Twentieth Century*, for "Writing for Myself," by permission of Harold Pinter and the editor.

From *Sartre*, by Iris Murdoch. By permission of Yale University Press.

Chronology

1930   October 10: born in Hackney, London, only son of a Jewish tailor, Hyman Pinter, and Frances Mann.

1939   Evacuated from London, first to Cornwall, then nearer home.

1944   Returns to London: Hackney Downs Grammar School. Plays Macbeth and Romeo in school productions.

1947   Leaves school.

1948-   LCC grant to study at the Royal Academy of Dramatic Art;
1949   leaves after a short time. Refuses National Service as a conscientious objector; fined on two occasions.

1949   Writing, mainly short stories and poems, including "Kullus."

1950   Two poems (by Harold Pinta) published in *Poetry London*. Begins work on an unpublished novel, *The Dwarfs*. First professional engagement as an actor in the BBC Home Service program on September 19, "Focus on Football Pools," followed on October 31 by "Focus on Libraries."

1951   January 14: plays the part of Abergavenny on BBC Third Program recording of *Henry VIII*. Attends Central School of Speech and Drama. September 1951 to autumn 1952: tours Ireland playing Shakespeare with Anew McMaster. *Poetry London* publishes another poem by Harold Pinta.

1953-   Acts with Donald Wolfit's company and in various provincial
1957   repertory companies (Colchester, Bournemouth, Torquay, Worthing, Richmond, and so on). First meeting with Vivien Merchant (Ada Thomson)

1954   Takes professional name of David Baron. Between engagements odd jobs such as waiter, doorman, dishwasher, and salesman.

1956   Marries Vivien Merchant while playing opposite her at Bournemouth.

1957   *The Room* produced by Drama Department, Bristol, then by Drama School of Bristol Old Vic. Pinter in repertory at Torquay; begins work on *The Birthday Party*. Recognized by Harold Hobson, drama critic of *The Sunday Times*. Michael Codron asks for any other plays he may have written: *The Party,* later *The Birthday Party*, and *The Dumb Waiter*. Acquires literary agent: Jimmy Wax.

1958 Son, Daniel, born. Moves to Chiswick. April 28: *The Birthday Party*. Well received on tour by Oxford and Cambridge audiences but lasts for only one week at the Lyric Opera House, Hammersmith. Harold Hobson defends the play in *The Sunday Times*, May 25. *The Hothouse* written but neither published nor performed. First attempt at a radio play, *Something in Common*, not performed but another play commissioned. October 27: BBC acknowledges receipt of *A Slight Ache*.

1959 February 28: *The Dumb Waiter* given its premiere in Germany. May 11: *The Birthday Party* produced by the Tavistock Players, Islington. July 29: *A Slight Ache* broadcast by the BBC Third Program. *A Night Out* written between July 7 and October 9; "The Examination" published in *Prospect* (Summer 1959). *Pieces of Eight*, Apollo Theatre, London, September 3, contains: "Getting Acquainted," "Request Stop," "Special Offer," and "Last to Go." *One to Another*, Lyric Opera House, Hammersmith, transferred to the Apollo Theatre, contains: "The Black and White" and "Trouble in the Works." December 10: *The Birthday Party* produced at the State Theatre, Braunschweig, Germany.

1960 January 21: *The Room* and *The Dumb Waiter* produced by Hampstead Theatre Club; transferred to the Royal Court Theatre in March. March 1: *A Night Out* broadcast by the BBC and televised in April. Pinter and Vivien Merchant appear in both productions. March 22: *The Birthday Party* televised. April 27: *The Caretaker* opens at the Arts Theatre Club, transferring to the Duchess Theatre on May 30 for a long run (425 performances), and wins Pinter the Evening Standard Award. July 21: *Night School* televised. July 27: First professional production of *The Birthday Party* in the United States by the Actors' Workshop in San Francisco. October 29: *Der Hausmeister* opens at the Düsseldorf Schauspielhaus. December 2: *The Dwarfs* broadcast on the BBC Third Program. (This play is now published in three versions, 1961, 1966, and 1968.)

1961 January 18: *A Slight Ache* performed as part of a triple bill with plays by N. F. Simpson and John Mortimer at the Arts Theatre Club. January 27: *Le Gardien* opens at the Théâtre de Lutèce, Paris. May 11: *The Collection* televised by Independent Television Authority. September 17: *A Night Out* staged at the Gate Theatre, Dublin. October 4: *The Caretaker* opens in New York with the London cast (apart from Robert Shaw, who replaced Peter Woodthorpe as Aston); wins Page One Award of the Newspaper Guild of New York.

1962   June 18: *The Collection* staged at the Aldwych by Peter Hall, beginning Pinter's association with the Royal Shakespeare Company. September 7: Pinter reads "The Examination" on the BBC Third Program. November: *The Servant*, directed by Joseph Losey, opens. December: filming *The Caretaker* begins at 31 Downs Road, Hackney, London.

1963   March 28: *The Lover* televised by Associated Rediffusion. Wins the Prix Italia for Television Drama at Naples; and Pinter, Alan Badel, and Vivien Merchant receive Guild of British Television Producers and Directors Awards for script and performances. Staged on September 18 with *The Dwarfs* at the Arts Theatre Club, Pinter directing *The Lover* and, assisted by Guy Vaesen, *The Dwarfs*. Completed filmscript *The Compartment* (which became *The Basement*). June 27: film version of *The Caretaker* opens at the Berlin Film Festival, winning one of the Silver Bears.

1964   March 2: screenplay of *The Servant* receives British Screenwriters Guild Award. February-March: nine revue sketches broadcast by the BBC Third Program. June 2: reads "Tea Party" on BBC Third Program. June 18: directs revival of *The Birthday Party* at the Aldwych Theatre.

1965   March: wins British Film Academy Award for best screenplay of 1964 for his adaptation of *The Pumpkin Eater*. *The Homecoming* starts its pre-London tour, opening at the Aldwych Theatre, June 3. March 25: *Tea Party* televised by BBC 1. October: first breakthrough in Paris with double bill of *The Collection* and *The Lover*. November 15: plays Garcia in Sartre's *Huis Clos* on BBC TV.

1966   June: awarded the CBE in the Birthday Honours List. October 11: *Le Retour* opens in Paris. November: premiere of *The Quiller Memorandum*, screenplay by Harold Pinter from *The Berlin Memorandum* by Adam Hall (Elleston Trevor). December 20: *The Homecoming* opens in Boston.

1967   January 3: *The Homecoming* opens in New York; wins the Tony Award for Best Play on Broadway; voted best play on

Broadway by the New York Drama Critics' Circle and received the Whitbread Anglo-American Award for the best British play on Broadway. February: first showing of *Accident*, screenplay by Pinter from the novel by Nicholas Mosley. February 28: *The Basement* broadcast on BBC TV with Pinter playing the role of Stott. July 27: Robert Shaw's play *The Man in the Glass Booth*, directed by Harold Pinter, opens in London. Pinter moves to a house near Regent's Park.

1968   *Landscape* not performed because of difficulties with the Lord Chamberlain; broadcast on April 25 by the BBC Radio Three. October 10: *Tea Party* and *The Basement* staged in New York at the East Side Playhouse. December 9: the film of *The Birthday Party* opens in New York.

1969   April 9: "Night" staged in *Mixed Doubles* at the Comedy Theatre. July 2: *Landscape* and *Silence* (completed in January) opens at the Aldwych Theatre. September 17: *Le Gardien* opens, again, in Paris, at the Théâtre Moderne. Screenplay for *The Go-Between* completed early in year.

1970   *Landscape* and *Silence* produced at the Forum Theater of the Lincoln Center, New York. *Tea Party* and *The Basement* staged at the Duchess Theatre. Awarded the Shakespeare Prize of the Freiherr v. Stein Foundation, Hamburg. Directs *Exiles*, by James Joyce, at the Mermaid Theatre.

1971   June 1: *Old Times* produced at the Aldwych Theatre in London, and in November in New York, where *The Birthday Party* and *The Homecoming* are also revived. The screenplay for *The Go-Between* receives an award at the Cannes Film Festival. Pinter directs *Butley* by Simon Gray at the Criterion Theatre. October: *C'était hier* opens at the Théâtre Montparnasse, Paris.

1972   Revival of *The Caretaker* at the Mermaid Theatre. Begins work on Proust. April 29: *Alte Zeiten* staged at the Thalia Theater, Hamburg.

1973   April 13: *Monologue* broadcast on BBC TV. Film version of *The Homecoming* by the American Film Theater. Autumn: appointed one of Peter Hall's Associate Directors at the National Theatre.

1975   April 23. *No Man's Land* opens at the National Theatre at the Old Vic, directed by Peter Hall; transfers on July 15 to Wyndham's Theatre. November 29: *Niemandsland* opens at the

Thalia Theater, Hamburg. December 3: *Monologue* broadcast by BBC Radio 3.

1978 November 15: *Betrayal* opens at the National Theatre.

1979 May 24: *Close of Play* by Simon Gray, directed by Harold Pinter at the National Theatre.

1980 May 1: *The Hothouse* opens at Hampstead Theatre in a production directed by Harold Pinter; later transfers to the Ambassadors Theatre. October 9: Pinter announces that he has married Lady Antonia Fraser; because of legal difficulties the marriage does not take place until November 27.

CHAPTER 1

The Pinter Problem

A CCORDING to Austin E. Quigley, writing in 1975, the problem is two-fold: first, where should criticism of Pinter go now after over a decade of criticism which has done nothing to advance our understanding of Pinter's work and continues to modify generalizations arrived at in the first few years of his career; and second, the audiences that rejected his particular kind of explicitness now appear to welcome it. All this second suggestion implies is that twenty years have made a difference to audiences if not to critics. It is not that audiences understand Pinter plays any better. They do, however, carry into the auditorium different expectations from those which they brought to the first production of *The Birthday Party*, and perhaps the critics should be given some credit for this. In fact the novelties of the late 1950s no longer strike us as novelties because we have grown used to them, and they now strike us as less revolutionary and more evolutionary. The particular kind of theater to which Pinter belonged was that in which two or three characters meet for the purpose of talking about themselves, and in his most recent play, *Betrayal*, we are still watching two or three people talking about themselves. In the early days of Pinter's career it seemed best to try to define his work with a label. It was— that early period of excitement and revolution—a period of labels— "Poetic," "Angry," "Absurd," and "Brechtian"—this last recognizing that there was a device called "Alienation" which also influenced physical aspects of staging.

It soon became clear that "Poetic" was inappropriate and it was replaced by "Verse"—the first revolt against the expectations of a paying audience in commercial theater. Until the early 1950s verse drama seemed the most hopeful trend to combat the stale and uncreative. It seemed to be a drama that was going somewhere. Its failure was probably due to the fact that these plays were the products of writers rather than dramatists, poetry *in* the theater rather than poetry *of* the theater. The difficulty was that the dramatists were not just writers but mainly poets who sought to widen their audiences by moving into the theater as much as enlarge the vocabulary of the drama by using the widest range of language, poetry, and thus capturing the fullest contrasts and the most intense moments of experience from which the moral lesson could emerge. T. S. Eliot was probably their most successful representative, arguing that poetic drama should not be an artificial world but one which would hopefully present "our own sordid, dreary daily world" which would be "suddenly illuminated and transfigured."[1] His first attempt, *Murder in the Cathedral,* avoided the difficulties since the audience was, in fact, a congregation used to ritual and fancy dress and elevated language. His first secular (contemporary) drama, *The Family Reunion* (1939), remains his only play that is uncompromisingly in verse and looks forward both to *Waiting for Godot* and *The Homecoming,* but thereafter we can trace a steady movement away from attempting nonrealistic action and from using verse for its originally stated purpose. It was, obviously, difficult if not impossible to combine in this day and age a natural action with dramatic blank verse. Commercial theater audiences naturally required the paraphernalia of life—telephones, umbrellas, and cocktails—and it is asking too much of an author that he produce verse of any intensity while answering the telephone, finding a lost umbrella, or mixing a cocktail, so the spectator comes to feel that these things are there simply to persuade him that, despite all evidence to the contrary, he is watching a play about a natural, contemporary matter. What began, then, as a powerful extension of drama into new areas of thought and expression declined into a mannerism.[2] But—and it is an important but—these plays did habituate audiences to new ideas about content and expression. They suggested that the theater was a place where serious matters could be discussed, and not necessarily in realistic terms. In this way they prepared audiences for both the Angry and Absurd Theaters.

I   *The "Angry" Theater*

"Angry" seemed, at the time, an appropriate label. Clearly Jimmy Porter in John Osborne's *Look Back in Anger* was angry, even if no one was particularly certain at what. Or was he? John Russell Taylor, who dated the new era in British theater from the production of this play in 1956, wrote of the ending of the play: "Faced at last with a really effective example of his own handiwork, Jimmy quails, and at last he and Alison are united again in their own idyllic dream world of bears and squirrels, content, perhaps, never to make it as human beings in the real world around." Nowadays critics are more likely to invoke D. H. Lawrence and Strindberg when discussing this play.

What John Osborne and the "Angries" did, however, was to break through into conventional theater by their sheer vitality, by using language that seemed contemporary (and often provincial), by encouraging young dramatists into believing that if they wrote plays they would be produced, and by showing that the theater was a place where contemporary problems could be discussed. Looking back at *Look Back in Anger* (1956), *The Entertainer* (1957), John Arden's *Live Like Pigs* (1958), and Wesker's first trilogy we can see that in spite of the ordinary people using ordinary language the plays are conventional, sentimental but still powerful. One should not dismiss Angry Theater too summarily, for it broke down a great number of barriers. Anger is essentially a dissolving emotion, and such plays were as useful and important as verse drama in widening the capabilities of an audience.

If Osborne was the most strident voice it was Arden and Wesker who seemed to have something important to say, who were "committed" playwrights. The problem of commitment has never been easy and hardly seems to concern us with Harold Pinter. As John Mander has pointed out, John Osborne's *Look Back in Anger* is a vehement play, but it is also noncommittal. Commitment cannot just mean party political involvement—any writer is obviously committed to a private quest for value in a valueless world: "Commitment is universal: the poet of subjectivity chooses to explore its inner rather than outer face."[3] Moreover commitment must be found in the art, not the artist, a distinction the modern critic finds hard to maintain. To confuse Jimmy Porter with his creator is plausible, even inevitable, but it is still mistaken.

In short, "Angry" Theater was neither more real, significant, nor committed than the plays of Beckett and Pinter. G. E. Wellwarth was probably correct when he suggested that British national pride was roused by the success of Osborne's play and overlooked the possibility that it was an accurate dissection of a perverse marriage in the style of Strindberg. He was certainly right when he considered what Hobson and Levin had said about Wesker and pointed out that Wesker's so-called working class is based on stock literary situations and caricature.[4] At first the Angry dramatists were traditionalists and only later came to graduate through self-conscious applications of Brechtian techniques to mature plays which include dream and fantasy. If there was a revolution, then, in British theater, it started a year earlier, in 1955, with the production of Beckett's *Waiting for Godot*.

II   *The Theater of the Absurd*

Beckett's play *Waiting for Godot* introduced English audiences to the kind of theater Martin Esslin has called "Absurd" and which Wellwarth dates precisely from December 10, 1896, with the first production of Alfred Jarry's *Ubu Roi*. From Jarry's play we move to the calculated insanity of 'Pataphysics, developed under Antonin Artaud into the spontaneous theater of "Cruelty" that reflects the condition of man faced with the unrelenting malignancy of incomprehensible cosmic powers that govern him. Absurd drama appears to have no social aim at all and the poetry of these plays is not in the language, which is kept deliberately flat and unpoetical, but in the action which Esslin dubbed "Absurd." Basically this kind of theater seeks to explore the feeling that the world cannot be explained or reduced to a system of values. Mr. Esslin relates this theater to contemporary trends in philosophy and, particularly, to that loose collection of philosophers called "Existentialist."

The essential characteristics of such plays are a preoccupation with failure, dread, and death. Such diverse figures as Kierkegaard, Dostoevsky, Nietzsche, Jaspers, Heidegger, Sartre, Rilke, and Kafka seem united in the perception of the absurdity of man's condition. Following in one direction from this perception (an important qualification since Pascal arrived at the same conclusion but it moved him in the opposite direction), Camus's book *The Myth of Sisyphus* contains the statement of belief: an absurd hero is punished with a futile and hopeless labor. Thus Esslin quotes Ionesco that man is lost, cut off from all his roots: "All his actions become senseless, absurd, useless."[5] This feeling is echoed in another quotation from Ionesco: "A curtain, an impassable wall stands between me and the world, between me and myself; matter fills every corner, takes up all the space and its weight annihilates all freedom; the horizon closes in and the world becomes a stifling dungeon. Language breaks down in a different way and words drop like stones or dead bodies; I feel I am invaded by heavy forces, against which I can only fight a losing battle."[6]

Noticeably this battle is with thought and the language with which to express thought; and the most detailed treatment of this process is in *Nausea* by Jean-Paul Sartre (itself influenced, even to the sickness image, by Rilke's "The Notes of Malte Laurids Brigge"). Pinter actually used the word "nausea" in a speech given to the Seventh National Drama Festival at Bristol in 1962, where, having described the pleasure in using words, he went on:

But at the same time I have another strong feeling about words which amounts to nothing less than nausea. Such a weight of words confronts us . . . words spoken . . . words written by me and others, the bulk of it stale, dead terminology, ideas endlessly repeated and permutated, become platitudinous, trite, meaningless. Given this nausea, it's very easy to be overcome by it and step back into paralysis. I imagine most writers know something of this kind of paralysis. But if it is possible to confront this nausea, to follow it to its hilt and move through it, then it is possible to say that something has occurred, that something has even been achieved.[7]

III   Nausea

Nausea is the diary of Roquentin in which he traces the growth of a sickness and the dissolution of the familiar world around him as the veneer of substance is stripped off and he arrives at truth:

And without formulating anything clearly, I understood that I had found the key to Existence, the key to my Nauseas, to my own life. In fact, all that I could grasp beyond that returns to this fundamental absurdity. Absurdity: another word; I struggle against words; down there I touched the thing. But I wanted to fix the absolute character of this absurdity here.[8]

As Iris Murdoch observes in her study of Sartre, Roquentin's metaphysical doubt is an old and familiar one: "The doubter sees the world of everyday reality as a fallen and bedraggled place, fallen out of the realm of being into the realm of existence. The circle does not exist; but neither does what is named as 'black' or 'table' or 'cold'! The relation of these words to their context of application is shifting and arbitrary. What *does* exist is brute and nameless, it escapes from the scheme of relations in which we imagine it to be rigidly enclosed, it escapes from language and science, it is more than and other than our description of it."[9] This is the realization that things which we recognize as stable, as having characteristics capable of being named, do not in fact have these qualities unambiguously. That the labels are fixed by the observer is, as Miss Murdoch suggests, one way of beginning philosophy, but is such a realization also a way of beginning drama?

Esslin certainly saw the label as useful in capturing the qualities of that drama, though he has since modified his position. Even so, in 1965, he continued to insist that such critical concepts were, albeit abused, still useful. Here, he pointed out, were plays that flouted the criteria of the well-made play but succeeded. The phrase "Theater of the Absurd" was a kind of "intellectual shorthand" to describe similarities and shared philosophical and artistic premises, whether conscious or not; and it helped to point to the central action of the play, action no longer inherent in a plot but in the unfolding of what he called a poetic image. Such images, he conceded, lack clarity but present strongly the loss of clear and well-defined beliefs. Man finds himself faced with a frightening and illogical universe, in which the means of communication, language, is suspect and, therefore, the well-made play with its "real" conversation is also suspect.

But there has been confusion in criticism about Absurdity. As F. N. Lees, writing about Beckett, has pointed out, the phrase has accuracy for Beckett only "as referring to the logician's *reductio ad absurdum,* a technique of demonstration, *not* a view of life."[10] In this sense Pinter may exhibit Absurdist tendencies. But if so he is nearer, say, Pirandello than Jarry. It is not so much the lack of logic as the madness of logic that informs the plays. Tynan, possibly swayed by his desire to defend committed art, seems for once to have missed the point when he writes: "Once having espoused the illogical, the irrelevant, the surreal, he [the Absurd dramatist] is committed; a single lapse into logic, relevance, or reality, and he is undone."[11] The relentless logic behind Absurdity is most evident in Pirandello, in a play like *The Rules of the Game* (1918), which almost sets a pattern for this kind of play.[12] Here a wife, estranged from her husband, tries to make it seem that she has been indecently approached by a young gallant who is also a brilliant duelist. She hopes that her husband, in fulfilling his conventional obligations, will get killed and leave her free to enjoy life with her lover. To her surprise, the husband not only issues the challenge but names her lover as his second. On the appointed day the husband simply stays in bed. He has issued the challenge (a nominal function) because he is her husband (a nominal function, too), but her lover (as the real husband) has to fight the duel (the real obligation) and is killed. Here the husband simply applies the rules of the game, logically.

Games of logic have been played frequently in contemporary drama: between husband and wife (Osborne's *Under Plain Cover,* Pinter's *The Lover,* or Albee's *Who's Afraid of Virginia Woolf?*);

between friends to pass the time (Beckett's *Waiting for Godot* or Pinter's *The Dumb Waiter*); or between strangers (Albee's *The Zoo Story*). What strikes the audience is that life may be a game but that game can be in deadly earnest. Indeed, much of the stichomythic dialogue such a situation requires is noticeably derived as much from music hall as classical French drama,[13] and this merging of comic and tragic—though symptomatic of contemporary drama—is no new development. J. L. Styan produces antecedents that include the Mystery plays, Euripides, Marlowe, Shakespeare and Molière, though it has to be observed that the mixture was less disturbing because it occurred in the context of an ethical convention denied to a contemporary audience. Recent drama has a habit of teasing and troubling an audience while it laughs—a device which Charney has labeled "tragic farce," where we need, for our own peace of mind, to postulate "a menacing reality hidden behind the staggering emptiness of everyday discourse."[14] That the audience no longer minds this, and even, indeed, feels cheated if it is not so disturbed, shows, again, a considerable shift in their expectations.

IV   *The Critics*

The expectations of audiences are a result partly of habit, but partly, too, a consequence of the critical endeavor of the last two decades. Professor Quigley accuses critics of Pinter of not progressing, of merely proliferating. This assumes that the basic ideas about his plays should develop and change. Now a dramatist, clearly, must develop and change but it is not, surely, necessary that assessment of his early plays should also develop and change? Or that a critic must have second thoughts when the first ones might be as right as possible? Still, the pressure to find a new approach appears irresistible.

Martin Esslin's *Pinter: A Study of His Plays* (published in its third, expanded edition in 1977) is a full treatment of the plays based on the dual nature of Pinter's work. The extreme naturalism of surface description and the dreamlike poetic feeling produce in the audience both amusement at the accuracy of observation and the unease "evoked by a subconscious response to the implications which spring from the author's own subconscious."[15] Thus, if Pinter lacks the sweep of a Brecht, Shaw, or Shakespeare, his importance rests of this fusion, on the depth of insights rather than the width of subject matter. This detailed treatment can also be found in Steven H. Gale's *butter's going*

up: a critical analysis of Harold Pinter's work (1977), which follows
up every clue exhaustively. On this base of line by line examination
other critics have been able to build their particular approaches. Thus
Walter Kerr (1967) saw Pinter as the only dramatist working in the
theater today who writes existentialist plays. Existentially man is born
undefined; we cannot say what a man is until we have seen how this
man actually behaves or what he has done. Man spends his time arriv-
ing at an identity which he only achieves at the moment of death. John
Russell Taylor (1969) pointed out that the urge to interpret is only natural—if a play tells a story there is a sense that it means more than it
says and the best a critic can do is to suggest continuity and expose the
mechanics of the play. Lois G. Gordon (also in 1969) advanced an early
Freudian interpretation. Pinter does not offer us Beckett's Everyman;
instead he focuses upon an everyman who exists in ordinary activity,
making decisions about the cornflakes and living in an emotional chaos
that is not a disorder born of cosmic or political confrontation but
rather the product of our everyday conflicts. The intruders, she suggests, are merely screens onto which are projected primitive and
repressed feelings hitherto submerged by the games. She sees Pinter as
neither Absurdist nor Existentialist but as a ruthless realist; his aim, like
Freud's, was "civilization and its discontents."[16]

This Freudian approach is more completely realized by Lucine P.
Gabbard in *The Dream Structure of Pinter's Plays* (1976). She dis-
claims any intention of psychoanalyzing Harold Pinter (Freud, after
all, insisted on the dreamer's cooperation!), but she hopes that treating
the plays as dreams can unlock many of their secrets. Her language is
dramatic (castration looms large; but a cigar, sometimes, is only a
cigar?) but curiously untheatrical. But her method does allow her to
say that Pinter's characters are motivated: "They are indeed motivated, as people in real life are motivated, by the psychological phe-
nomena of the unconscious. Approaching Pinter's plays as a dream has
provided a glimpse of the psychological realities of life."[17] The feeling
remains, however, that Pinter, his characters, and the audience are all
being psychoanalyzed; but it would be churlish to deny that the book
does provide insights.

The realm of the unconscious, however, is probably more plausibly
interpreted by William Baker and Stephen E. Tabachnik (1973). They
are both lecturers in English at the University of the Negev in Israel
and present the Jewish point of view, one so obvious that it is surprising
it took so long in coming. They take as the basis of their investigation

Pinter's reticence about his own life which has concealed the fact that "at bottom, he is fascinated by the concrete world of his private history" and that his work is an ever-continuing dialogue between past and present, stemming from a Jewish childhood in Hackney.[18] Meanwhile the sense of ritual in Pinter was explored by Katherine H. Burkman (1973), who contends that beneath the daily rituals "beat the rhythms of ancient fertility rites, which form a significant counterpoint to the surface rituals of the plays and which often lend the dramas their shape and structure."[19] Here Frazer's Golden Bough offers a clue to the *metaphorical* (my italics) ritual sacrifice which is at the center of Pinter's drama.

One can quite understand why Austin E. Quigley is mistrustful of all these critical alternatives—allegory, dream, metaphor, and above all the subtext which he suggests does not exist. His Golden Bough is linguistics, and his rituals are laid down by Wittgenstein, J. R. Firth, and M. A. K. Halliday. Unfortunately he produces no new insights and he seems largely unaware that he is dealing with plays. The fact is that the idea of a subtext is very valuable in dealing with the theater, which is the spoken word, not the written word; as is the recognition that theater language is not simply verbal. Evasive though these resorts to allegory, and phrases like what is said beneath, above, and below the line, are, they are not dishonest; they seek genuinely to convey performance, and that curious dualism which performance invariably produces. The *Observer* Profile (September 15, 1963) saw Pinter as two people: "One is the dramatist who built up an imaginatively self-sufficient world out of fragments of common life often disregarded by other writers, and introduced a new type of theatrical poetry based on Cockney speech patterns. The other is a swarthy, vigorous ex-repertory actor with a tough, down-to-earth manner that would make him at home in a boxing gym or dockside pub." We need to recognize the apparent contradiction. Pinter, it is true, can *seem* very existential. In his article "Between the Lines" (*The Sunday Times*, March 4, 1962) he wrote of the impossibility of verifying the past—even yesterday or this morning!—the dangers of communication, and the impossibility of making a final or definitive statement: "No statement I make, therefore, should be interpreted as final or definitive. One or two of them may sound final and definitive, but I won't regard them as such tomorrow and I wouldn't like you to do so today." But in reading this we are struck, surely, as much by his sense of humor as anything else. Which is not to deny that he is serious. In writing plays he most certainly is:

No, I'm not committed as a writer, in the usual sense of the term, either religiously or politically. And I'm not conscious of any particular social function. I write because I want to write. I don't see any placards on myself, and I don't carry any banners. Ultimately I distrust any definitive labels. . . . The old categories of comedy and tragedy and farce are irrelevant, and the fact that managers seem to have realised that is one of the favorable changes. But writing for the stage is the most difficult thing of all, whatever the system. I find it more difficult the more I think about it.[20]

CHAPTER 2

Language and Silence

T HE plays of Harold Pinter are not obviously (as with Osborne and Wesker) a kind of spiritual autobiography, but as biography has been filled in, our sense of the plays has been enlarged. Whether or not we accept Baker/Tabachnik's interpretation of the plays as confessions of a hidden Jew who grew up in Hackney we cannot avoid some suggestions. Barry Supple, a school friend of Pinter's, writing in the *Jewish Chronicle* has described a Pinter play as "a great echo chamber in which the only sources of sound are the prosaic data of the dramatist's life history but in which nearly all the sounds are magnified and distorted into bizarre and sometimes shocking combinations."[1] Journalists and critics have continued to pile up details—some of them very odd indeed—thus we were told that the Pinter loo had a footpedal instead of a chain (*Nova*, September 1967)—but the dangers are obvious. Pinter ruefully reflected in his Hamburg Speech of 1970 on the famous phrase about the weasel under the cocktail cabinet which he referred to with no thought at all and to frustrate further enquiry and which has now acquired profound significance. How far, for example, are we to see in plays after 1975 signs of the breakdown of his marriage to Vivien Merchant?

Certainly the experience as an actor between 1950–57 forms the basis for his sense of stagecraft and his themes: " Continuous migration, the unsettled actor's life involving bit parts and shabby digs, reinforce the tone of uncertainty in his work. Digs at Eastbourne form the setting of *The Birthday Party*, experience as a caretaker in Notting Hill Gate contributes to *The Caretaker*. But the complexes and impulses which give the deepest power to his creative impetus lie in the early years, that foreign country which continually comes to the surface in his later work."[2] Odd jobs, including doorman, snow shoveler, street salesman, dance hall bouncer surface tantalizingly in his plays. Even his love of cricket ("Every time we evacuated, I took my cricket bat with me"— *New Yorker*, February 25, 1967) can suggest camouflage, to hide his

Jewishness. Biography is dangerous, but it can no longer be ignored. One obvious seminal source stems from growing up as a Jew in the East End of London: violence and anti-Semitism. Wesker, another local lad, has dramatized the events of October 4, 1936 (see *Chicken Soup with Barley*) when the fascists planned to march to Aldgate down Commercial Road to Salmon Lane in Limehouse and hold a meeting in the center of the Jewish area, Victoria Park. The Second World War did not remove these tensions:

If you looked remotely like a Jew you might be in trouble. Also, I went to a Jewish club, by an old railway arch, and there were quite a lot of people often waiting with broken milk bottles in a particular alley we used to walk through. There were one or two ways of getting out of it—one was a purely physical way, of course, but you couldn't do anything about the milk bottles—we didn't have any milk bottles. The best way was to talk to them, you know, sort of "Are you all right?" "Yes, I'm all right." "Well, that's all right, then isn't it?" And all the time keep walking toward the lights of the main road. . . . There was a good deal of violence there, in those days.[3]

This episode illustrates two basic things about Pinter: themes and technique; politics and language.

I Politics

Politics and Pinter still seem unconnected. The *Observer* Profile pointed out how sensitive he was to being regarded as one of a group, that he had voted only once (Labour) and regretted that as a sentimental gesture and he refused to be billed as a Royal Court playwright. In the Bensky interview he maintains that politics do bore him, though he recognizes that they can cause a great deal of suffering; and he is on record as saying:

I find most political thinking and terminology suspect, deficient. It seems to me a dramatist is entitled to portray the political confusion in a play if his characters naturally act in a political context, that is, if the political influences operating on them are more significant than any other considerations. But I object to the stage being used as a substitute for the soap box where the author desires to make a direct statement at all costs, and forces his characters into fixed and artificial postures in order to achieve this. This is hardly fair on the characters. I don't care for the didactic or moralistic theater. In England I find this theater, on the whole, sentimental and unconvincing.[4]

Yet he did state, in *Vogue* (October 1964), that he was categorically anti the Americans in Vietnam and strongly in favor of Israel, and his name did appear among the sponsors for the Angry Arts Week in 1967, and as early as 1960, in an interview with Kenneth Tynan, he conceded that his characters might have listened to a political meeting and even voted, but:

> I'm dealing with these characters at the extreme edge of their living, where they are living pretty much alone, at their hearth, their home hearth. . . . We all, I think . . . may have sexual relationships or go to political meetings or discuss ideas, but when we get back to our rooms and we are faced with a bed and we are either alone or with someone else, then. . . . I don't think we go on long about ideas or political allegiances . . . I mean, there comes a point, surely, where this living in *the* world must be tied up with living in *your own* world, where you are—in your room. . . . Before you manage to adjust yourself to living alone in your room . . . you are not terribly fit and equipped to go out and fight the battles . . . which are fought mostly in abstractions in the outside world.[5]

This existential adjustment, as many critics have pointed out, is not a philosophical abstraction but based on the experience of a Jewish boy in the East End of London growing up in the Europe of Hitler and facing basic political problems about power, cruelty, terror: *Lebensraum*. When Pinter became eligible for National Service he declared himself a conscientious objector. Two tribunals rejected his application and he was fined twice for refusing to obey his call-up papers: "I was aware of the suffering and of the horror of war, and by no means was I going to subscribe to keeping it going."[6] He could have been sent to prison for this commitment. So there is more than a hint of political and social problems and a hatred of violence. And one of the stratagems to cope with it, as the milk bottle episode illustrates, was language and manners.

II *Language*

Austin E. Quigley makes heavy weather of the milk bottle episode but we do not really need Wittgenstein to help us out here. Indeed the description of that episode as a verbal event gives the game away, Pinter's language is dramatic, it fulfils Brecht's insistence that language should be gestural (i.e. forcing, by syntax and rhythm, the appropriate gestures on an actor). And it is not a matter of communication so much

as mediation. Communication, Pinter feels, would be too alarming. So
Pinter uses the two silences:

There are two silences. One when no word is spoken. The other when perhaps
a torrent of language is employed. This speech is speaking of a language
locked beneath it. That is its continual reference. The speech we hear is an
indication of what we don't hear. It is a necessary avoidance, a violent, sly,
anguished or mocking smokescreen which keeps the other in its place. When
true silence falls we are still left with echo but are nearer nakedness. One way
of looking at speech is to say it is a constant strategem to cover nakedness.[7]

Thus silence is used in two ways; technical and thematic. The technical
usage appears on every page in every play, with the liberal appearance
of "silence" and "pause." Martin Esslin has defined the difference
between the two, but a more sensitive description occurs in Dirk
Bogarde's *Snakes and Ladders:*

There is a popular and far too widely-held belief among many actors, and
directors too (not to mention critics) that Pinter writes pauses. I don't think
that he does. But I do think that he is one of the few writers who are brilliant
in the text they *don't* write. His pauses are merely the time-phases which he
gives you so that you may develop the thought behind the lines he has written, and to alert your mind itself to the dangerous simplicities of the lines to
come.[8]

Behind, beneath the lines are ways of describing how silence works for
Pinter. Just as the reticent Pinter needs a closed, framed stage where
characters can be shut away and spied on, so the subtext is an essential
part of Pinter's use of language. Explaining his characters Pinter has
said: "Between my lack of biographical data about them and the
ambiguity of what they say there lies a territory which is not only worthy of exploration but which it is compulsory to explore. You and I,
the characters which grow on a page, most of the time we're inexpres-
sive, giving little away, unreliable, elusive, obstructive, unwilling. But
it's out of these attributes that a language arises. A language . . . where,
under what is said, another thing is being said."[9] Pinter explores the
pleasure of language and the inadequacy of language, and the inter-
play between the two provides the tension in his stage dialogue.
Clearly, mention of the subtext recalls Chekhov the dramatist and
Stanislavski the director. Stanislavski believed that words without realization by actors of the subtext had no excuse for being presented on

stage. But Pinter has not freed his actors to bring their own notions and virtuosity to their parts: "There are certain limits on the actors set by what I write: they can enjoy themselves, but not in the way that Wolfit or McMaster enjoyed themselves."[10] However Pinter merely continues the obscure dialogue found in Chekhov or, for that matter, in Strindberg, who wrote in the preface to *Miss Julie:*

Finally, the dialogue. Here I have somewhat broken with tradition by not making my characters catechists who sit asking stupid questions in order to evoke some witty retort. I have avoided the symmetrical, mathematically constructed dialogue of the type favoured in France, and have allowed their minds to work irregularly, as people's do in real life, when, in conversation, no subject is fully exhausted, but one mind discovers in another a cog which it has a chance to engage. Consequently, the dialogue, too, wanders, providing itself in the opening scenes with matter which is later taken up, worked upon, repeated, expanded and added to, like the theme of a musical composition.[11]

Quigley has little patience with such analogies, condemning these resorts to poetry, subtext or music as critical failures:

They encourage poorly controlled impressionistic statements instead of demonstrably accurate analytic statements. The things they deal with are either linguistically specified or they are not there, and if they are linguistically specified, they are available for analysis and demonstration. The unanalysed in Pinter's work is a product of temporary critical failure, not of some metaphysical, ultra-valuable, unanalyzable characteristic located behind, above, or beneath the text of the plays.[12]

But the trouble is that these words operate in a theater, not on a page: we go to the theater to see a play, not to listen to it, and that is not a linguistic muddle. He keeps on saying that it is generally recognized that Pinter is doing something new with language, which is itself contentious, and his insistence on demonstration and analysis overlooks the context: the theater, where language is not primarily verbal. Naturalism had imposed severe restrictions on the resources of the word in the theater to which a recognition of its inadequacy adds a new dimension. Verse drama had sought to redress the balance—but reliance on words alone had limited it. Eliot could not understand how Ibsen achieved certain effects in prose which Eliot had believed could only be achieved by poetry! The subtext, admittedly, was only Stanislavski's

way of teaching an actor how to speak the words of a play, particularly
those by Chekhov, but since then a text in the theater has been either
pretext or scenario. Gordon Craig discovered a clue to the art of the
theater when he saw a notice in Munich theater: *Sprechen streng ver-
boten*. Yet, Beckett and Pinter are immensely literary. How then does
Pinter resolve the tension between spontaneity and design, between
silence and speech, between ordinary conversation and the need to say
everything in two hours? Andrew Kennedy describes Pinter's solution
as mannerist: "an inherent and consistent tendency to exploit 'conceits,'
linguistic complexity or modish *jeux d'esprit*, which a 'sophisticated'
public can be expected to understand and enjoy."[13] Such a style
requires a trained audience (which Pinter now has) and relies on classical forms (that is, it exploits known forms such as the thriller or the
drawing room comedy). Often such a style becomes too self-regarding,
but this, Kennedy feels, is a small price to pay for the results, a new
kind of expressiveness in a theater of language. It is precisely this quality to which Trussler, *inter alia*, objects. He feels Pinter cannot survive
as a dramatist because he writes for the times and the actors who act
in them. His assessment is that Pinter is not interested in what is being
said, but only how, and is, therefore, God's gift to the acting profession.
But the plays are *about* something, and if that something is manners
we still enjoy the plays of Congreve, Wilde, and Coward and still
encourage actors to perform them correctly. And Pinter falls into that
comic tradition.

III   *Beckett (and/or Coward)*

Surprisingly Pinter is much translated; Martin Esslin lists French,
German, Czech, Spanish, Dutch, Italian, Portuguese, Serbo-croat,
Turkish, Danish, Hungarian, Swedish, and Polish. I say "surprisingly"
because his kind of vernacular dialogue, conversational, idiomatic,
seems as English as cricket and ought not to translate at all.[14] We associate Pinter with Beckett and Kafka, but listening to his dialogue we
ought also to connect him with Wilde and Coward. Coward has always
praised Pinter: he spoke warmly of *The Caretaker* in *The Sunday
Times* (January 15, 1961), and in the *Sunday Telegraph* (May 22,
1966) he wrote:

Pinter is a very curious, strange element. He uses language marvellously well.
He is what I would call a genuine original. Some of his plays are a little

obscure, a little difficult, but he's a superb craftsman, creating atmosphere with words that sometimes are violently unexpected.

Katherine Worth has pointed out that Pinter's characters tend to fall into Coward-like groups—the good actors and the not so good; and that style is "used as a weapon and a facade in much the way that it is by Coward's glib over-articulate and amoral creatures."[15]

The connection with Beckett is more immediate and obvious. It is not just that Beckett was very much in the air when Pinter came on the scene—the differences are obvious—but Pinter has acknowledged a debt and an admiration. Asked by Bensky about literary influences Pinter replied that Beckett and Kafka stayed with him most: "I think Beckett is the best prose writer living"[16] and his contribution to the Festschrift for Beckett at Sixty (1967) ended with the lines: "Well, I'll buy his goods, hook, line and sinker, because he leaves no stone unturned and no maggot lonely. He brings forth a body of beauty. His work is beautiful." Pinter discovered the novels of Beckett in 1949 when an extract from *Watt* was published in *Irish Writing* and he was so enthusiastic that he stole a copy of *Murphy* from Bermondsey Public Library. When *Watt* was published in 1953 he read the whole book.[17] According to an interview in the *New York Times* (November 18, 1971) Pinter habitually sent each new play in manuscript to Beckett in the late 1960s before anyone else was allowed to see it, remarking that "he writes the most succinct observations." But Pinter's plays are different; they move forward while Beckett is cyclic and static. A Pinter character can always be taken out of the play and traditional reasons for his existence discussed, and there is little, if any, of Beckett's intense metaphysical anguish. What anguish there is is rooted in Pinter's life and times in Hackney, on the road to Regent's Park.

CHAPTER 3

Comedies of Menace

T HE title of this chapter was first applied to Pinter by Irving Wardle in *Encore* (September 1958), though it had appeared as the
subtitle of a play by David Campton called *The Lunatic View* in 1957.
Campton explicitly devoted the Absurd to social comment—as a
weapon against complacency and in his "sick" comedies the source of
menace is clear enough. In Pinter it has been universalized without
losing its power. Pinter's terror is outside every door. In the "Tempo"
program about his adolescence in Hackney Pinter denied that the
atmosphere of violence was attributable to his Jewishness, though that
must have contributed to his recognition of it. Trussler has objected to
the use of "comedy" on the grounds that comedy throws into relief the
eccentricities of everyday life whereas Pinter's plays are too devoid of
social setting; but his alternative—tragic farce—seems no better. In
fact the early plays have more precise settings than appeared at first,
and if Pinter's themes are loneliness, menace, communication, and verification, his characteristic mode of expression is comedy, though, as
Alrene Sykes aptly remarks, that comedy is frequently built "on the
quicksands of fear."[1] Either description reminds us of the mixed nature
of the plays—comedy that causes pain, and the peculiar misery of
changing sides during the action, which in retrospect is hardly as novel
as it seemed at the time. And since Pinter seldom stands still, but
always develops, the first plays are the best place to start, those plays
written about 1957 which enjoyed little success: *The Room, The Birthday Party,* and *The Dumb Waiter.*

   All the time Pinter was acting (or "resting") he was writing, not
plays but poems and short prose pieces, many of which were in dialogue form and anticipated his revue sketches, and the plays. He also
wrote a novel based on his youth in Hackney which was never published but which later appeared transformed into *The Dwarfs.* The
basic form for Pinter remains a series of images which, as Esslin
observes, "never aspire to be arguments, explanations or even coherent

stories."[2] His plays do, however, seem to be constantly aspiring to the condition of a poem!

I *Poetry*

Some of his poems were published, particularly in *Poetry London*, where they are sometimes ascribed to a Harold Pinta.[3] A selection by Alan Clodd was published by the Enitharmon Press in 1968 and in 1978 Methuen published *Poems and Prose: 1949–1977*, selected by the author and dedicated to Antonia Fraser. It is difficult to judge these poems without taking into account Pinter's successes elsewhere. They could not fail to be interesting, and critics have found in them all the characteristic themes: "the relativity of truth, mortality, dreams, the past, the intruder, dominance and subservience, and the sexual condition of men and women," though the techniques are fairly orthodox.[4] The early poems have echoes of Dylan Thomas, though they are mainly concerned with low-life in the city, as in "New Year in the Midlands," published in November 1950, which suggests that Pinter already has his themes and a great delight in language:

> Now here again she blows, landlady of lumping
> Fellows between the boards.
> Singing "O Celestial Light," while
> Like a T-square on the
> Flood swings her wooden leg.
> This is the shine, the powder and blood and here am I,
> Straddled, exile always in one Whitbread Ale town,
> Or such.
> Where we went to the yellow pub, cramped in an alley bin,
> A shoot from the market,
> And found the thin Luke of a queer, whose pale
> Deliberate eyes, raincoat, Victorian,
> Sap the answer in the palm.
> All the crush, camp, burble and beer
> Of this New Year's Night; the psalm derided;
> The black little crab women with the long
> Eyes, lisp and claw in a can of chockfull stuff.
> I am rucked in the heat of treading; the wellrolled
> Sailor boys soon rocked to sleep, whose ferret fig
> So calms the coin of a day's fever.
> Now in this quaver of a roisty bar, the wansome lady

I blust and stir,
Who pouts the bristle of a sprouting fag—
Sprinkled and diced in these Midland lights
Are Freda the whimping glassy bawd, and your spluttered guide,
Blessed with ambrosial bitter weed.—Watch
How luminous hands
Unpin the town's genitals—
Young men and old
With beetle glance,
The crawing brass whores, the clamping
Red shirted boy, ragefull, thudding his cage.

More obviously significant is the prose poem *Kullus* (1949), where the
narrator allows an outsider, Kullus, into his room. Kullus at once starts
to take over, calling in a girl who is waiting outside and without paus-
ing they climb into the narrator's bed. Before long the girl invites the
narrator to reverse the roles and the characters of the narrator and
Kullus seem to blur; the past blurs, too, in a mysterious and ambiguous
present. This sets the pattern of room, intruder, possession, but also the
suggestion that in seeking the comfort of a room a young man gives up
the chance of a girl. It was the first set of ideas, however, that occurs
in the early plays which, Pinter claims, grew imaginatively out of a
situation or image:

I went into a room one day and saw a couple of people in it. This stuck with
me for some time afterwards, and I felt that the only way I could give it
expression and get it off my mind was dramatically. I started off with this
picture of two people and let them carry on from there. It wasn't a deliberate
switch from one kind of writing to another. It was quite a natural movement.
A friend of mine, Henry Woolf, produced the result—*The Room*—at Bristol
University, and a few months later in January 1958 it was included—in a
different production—in the Festival of University drama. Michael Codron
heard about the play and wrote to me at once to ask if I had a full-length
play. I had just finished *The Birthday Party.* . . .

II   The Room

The Room was written in four days and begins with what Pinter
saw as a very potent question: what is going to happen to these two
people in a room? Will someone come in? Noticeably Pinter is equally
aware of the image as both verbal and visual: "I see things pretty

clearly, certainly, but I am continually surprised by what I see and by what suddenly happens in the play while I am writing it. I do not know, however, that the visual is more important to me than the verbal, because I am pretty well obsessed with words when they get going. It is a matter of tying the words to the image of the character standing on the stage. The two things go very closely together."[5] The words, as has been frequently recognized, are the language of cliché, but concentrated and organized so that the short period of the play produces the fullest impact on an audience. If the language is naturalism it is very much orchestrated naturalism. *The Room* contains the style, setting, and themes for Pinter's work up to and including *The Caretaker*, and noticeably the language is used to conceal rather than reveal. Pinter enlarged upon the initial image in *Time* (November 10, 1961) when he recalled seeing two men at a party—the little man feeding an enormous lorry driver with bread and butter and talking all the while. This image has been translated into Rose and Bert. In a shabby room in a large house, Rose, a woman of sixty, is fussing over her husband, Bert, a man of fifty, a van driver, who appears to be rather simple-minded but who never speaks to her, not even to reply to her monologue on the virtues of the room they live in. Outside the weather is cold and wintry (the second line of the play is, ominously, "It's murder"). Pinter is already *using* weather, here to emphasize the protective envelope or womb the room appears to provide for the characters. Rose's motherly solicitude for Bert is *partly* justified by the fact (?), suggested later in the play, that he has been ill; and her praise of the room is *partly* justified by the later suggestion that they have just moved into the area, though neither of these "facts" can be taken as necessarily true or false. The room for Rose is comfortable, representing, as it does, her only security; and it is just right for her—it is not in the basement (which is cold and damp) nor too far up. Also nobody bothers them:

This is a good room. You've got a chance in a place like this. I look after you, don't I, Bert? Like when they offered us the basement here I said no straight off. I knew that'd be no good. The ceiling right on top of you. No, you've got a window here, you can move yourself, you can come home at night, if you have to go out, you can do your job, you can come home, you're all right. And I'm here. You stand a chance.[6]

Pinter's plays are about people bothering people who want to keep to themselves; who find communication too alarming. The first intruder is the landlord, Mr. Kidd, who arrives, talks, but tells us nothing. He and Rose do, however, confirm each other's opinion that this room is the best in the house—the downstairs is damp and upstairs the rain comes in. But even Mr. Kidd seems vague about the extent of the house—which room was what in the past—and his own parentage since he cannot decide whether his mother was a Jewess or not. Although he suggests that the house is full at the moment he also says that he can take his pick of the rooms for his own bedroom. When he leaves, he is followed out a little later by the silent Bert. Rose begins to tidy up, but on opening the door to empty the garbage can, she finds a young couple in the dark on the landing and invites them in. Clarissa and Toddy Sands are looking for a room and have been told that there is one vacant in the house, but they have been unable to find the land-lord or explore the house, which is in darkness. As a married couple (presumably) they, too, seem on edge with each other; indeed the ver-bal battles between these two introduce a note of comedy into the play, though it is tinged with unease. They, for example, know the landlord by another name; and their bickering over whether Toddy should or should not sit down, whether Clarissa did or did not see a star, makes for uneasy laughter. When Toddy accidentally does sit down, Clarissa pounces:

MRS. SANDS: You're sitting down.
MR. SANDS: *(jumping up)*:   Who is?
MRS. SANDS: You were.
MR. SANDS: Don't be silly. I perched.
MRS. SANDS: I saw you sit down.
MR. SANDS: You did not see me sit down because I did not sit bloody well down. I perched!
MRS. SANDS: Do you think I can't perceive when someone's sitting down?
MR. SANDS: Perceive! That's all you do. Perceive.
MRS. SANDS: You could do with a bit more of that instead of all that tripe you get up to.
MR. SANDS: You don't mind some of that tripe!
MRS. SANDS: You take after your uncle, that's who you take after!
MR. SANDS: And who do you take after?
MRS. SANDS *(rising:)*   I didn't bring you into the world.
MR. SANDS: You didn't what?
MRS. SANDS: I said, I didn't bring you into the world.
MR. SANDS: Well, who did then? That's what I want to know. Who did? Who did bring me into the world?[7]

Even if we do not accept Gabbard's contention that this episode can be interpreted as penis envy and the desire to castrate it does contain arguments and fears that are still reverberating in the last plays; yet the mysteries seem irrelevant to the plot here and now, and indeed these exchanges delay the information that Rose desperately wants: which room is vacant? It turns out that a man sitting in the dark in the basement has told the Sandses that Room Seven is vacant. Since this is Rose's room she is naturally alarmed and gets rid of the couple, but Mr. Kidd bursts in. While she tries to question him about her room and what the Sandses told her, he, too, tries to tell her something, something he can only tell her when Bert is away. This information *partly* explains the inconsequential nature of his first visit but raises further questions in doing so—namely, why must Bert be out of the way before he can tell her? There is, he says, a man in the basement who is waiting to see her, who will not go away without seeing her, and who just sits there waiting, not even willing to play a game of chess to pass the time. Rose is finally convinced that she must see the stranger because he might turn up when Bert was there (again, why her panic?), so, she tells Mr. Kidd to send him up quickly. A blind Negro enters (so sitting in the dark is explained?) who says that his name is Riley and whom Rose immediately attacks for upsetting her landlord. But her dialogue contains one or two curious phrases—"you're all deaf, dumb and blind, *the lot of you*"; "oh, these *customers*" (italics mine)—that are obscure. And why does Rose deny that his name could be Riley? Her harangue culminates in a denial that is also a request:

ROSE: You've got what? How could you have a message for me, Mister
        Riley, when I don't know you and nobody knows I'm here and I
        don't know nobody anyway. You think I'm an easy touch, don't
        you? Well, why don't you give it up as a bad job? Get off out of it.
        I've had enough of this. You're not only a nut, you're a blind nut
        and you can get out the way you came. *Pause.* What message?
        Who have you got a message from? Who?
RILEY: Your father wants you to come home.[8]

The Negro repeats this message, calling her "Sal"—a name she does not deny; indeed, since she says, "Don't call me that," she almost admits to it. As she is feeling his face with her fingers (the action of a blind person rather than of a seeing one), Bert returns. He describes, in one short, violent speech, his furious drive back, how the one car that got in his way got "bumped," and how the van (which is feminine) goes well with him. Then he sits down and looks at the Negro for a few minutes. Suddenly he throws the Negro on the floor with the single word: "Lice." Then Bert beats him to death against the gas stove while Rose screams and announces that she is blind.

III   *Criticism of* The Room

The Room drew an admiring notice from Harold Hobson at its performance at Bristol University and *The Times* compared Pinter to Webern because both incline "to etiolated pointilliste textures, forever trembling on the edge of silence, and to structures elusive, yet so precisely organised that they possess an inner tension nonetheless potent because its sources are not completely understood."[9] If the play is not finally successful the fault lies in its melodramatic ending and the portentous Negro. Such a character inevitably invites a symbolic response—is he Death, the woman's past, or some hidden guilt?—summarized by Esslin as follows:

He has been lying down below and had foreknowledge of the future—that room number seven would soon be vacant—he must therefore be a being from beyond the confines of this world: a dead man or a messenger of death, perhaps Rose's own dead father. His blackness and blindness reinforce these allegorical implications. The blindness which strikes Rose at the end belongs to the same category of symbolism—it must mean the end of her relationship with Bert, but probably more than that: her own death.[10]

But Esslin supports this by transferring Bert's sexual energy to the van—which, surely, overlooks the fact that they are sixty and fifty, respectively.

Quigley has little sympathy for this interpretation of the Negro as a symbol of anything: he sees the process of adjustment as central to the play, not a symbol or message. The Negro is not merely feared but also desired by Rose and the play explores both fear and curiosity, change and resistance to change. But the appearance of the Negro is too suggestive to be simply ignored. As Clifford Leech astutely remarked, we are "conscious of being invited to look for allegory and yet not sufficiently impelled to conduct the search,"[11] while Trussler has pointed out that in a physical sense at least this Negro is nonsymbolic: he is black and blind—so we sense Pinter's Jewishness in the subtext. Rose is recalled to her race, and her father might even be Irish. At any rate the mixture of an Irish name and a black face makes Riley an ideal image for the "foreign" that so terrifies Pinter characters; and if he is a cousin to the One Eyed Reilly who appears as a means of redemption in T. S. Eliot's *The Cocktail Party* then his daughter has had a very full sex life indeed!

Some puzzles can be explained (a blind man sits in the dark) and some motives can be provided (Sal has become Rose and as Sal she led a life which would appall Bert). Mr. Kidd's musings about his Jewish origins are, however, mechanical—suggesting he is either a liar, a deliberate mystifier, or, perhaps, just forgetful in old age? Is the father from whom the message comes the kind of Father we meet in T. S. Eliot? Intruders are repelled, but has a room which stifles any value? The imagery of warm/cold, light/dark which runs through the play might mean something. We cannot, however, complain of and praise the multiple possibilities simultaneously, though it is human nature to do so. The basic Pinter device of contradiction appears here in full play: "The technique of casting doubt upon everything by matching each apparently clear and unequivocal statement with an equally clear and unequivocal statement of its contrary . . . is one which we shall find used constantly in Pinter's plays to create an air of mystery and uncertainty."[12]

If the suppression of motive is often arbitrary the central theme, surely, is that even one who acts cannot know what impels action. A Freudian interpretation may provide insights, but they will be no more valuable than Stanislavski's specifics. The question being asked is: can we ever know the truth about anyone or anything? Is there, in fact, an absolute truth to be known? In *The Room* it is not so much, we feel, that motives are unknowable as that the author will not let us know them. The play remains a good piece of theater, if weak as drama: the final explosion occurs rapidly, stunning the audience. But the mature Pinter said he would have had the characters sit down and drink a cup of tea—which is even more disturbing.

IV   The Birthday Party

Pinter recalls that *The Birthday Party* was written while he was touring in some kind of farce:

It was sparked off from a very distinct situation in digs when I was on tour. In fact the other day a friend of mine gave me a letter I wrote him in nineteen-fifty something. Christ knows when it was. This is what it says, "I have filthy insane digs, a great bulging scrag of a woman with breasts rolling at her belly, an obscene household, cats, dogs, filth, teastrainers, mess, oh bullocks, talk, chat, rubbish shit scratch dung poison, infantility, deficient order in the upper fretwork, fucking roll on. . . ." Now the thing about this is *that* was *The Birthday Party*—I was in those digs, and this woman was Meg in the play, and there was a fellow staying there in Eastbourne, on the coast. The whole thing remained with me, and three years later I wrote the play.[13]

Before we "explain" in terms of allegory and symbol we should perhaps consider that it might simply be true. Audiences certainly could not, and although it was successful at the Arts Theatre in Cambridge it was disastrously unsuccessful when it was presented at the Lyric in Hammersmith.

The Birthday Party opens with another breakfast scene, this time at the Boles's. Meg and Petey Boles live in a run-down boarding house at the seaside (Petey is apparently a deck-chair attendant), and they have only one guest, Stanley. The opening scene is reminiscent of both *The Room* (Meg mothers Petey and hates going out) and *The Dumb Waiter* (which also starts with items read out from a newspaper). From the news items read out by Petey—that Lady Mary Splatt has had a baby, a girl—emerges the possible fact that Meg needs a son and that the lodger, Stanley, fills that role as well as that of a young lover. Petey announces the possible arrival of two new guests, and Meg goes up to waken Stanley—a noisy game from which she appears panting and rearranging her hair. Stanley enters "unshaven, in his pyjama jacket and wearing glasses." Over breakfast he teases Meg—calling her fried bread "succulent," a word she is certain is an improper comment on herself. Stanley, apparently, was a great concert pianist stopped short in his career by "them." He is alarmed and unbelieving when told that two new guests are coming and pretends, with ironic cruelty, that they will cart Meg away in a wheelbarrow.

A young girl, Lulu, who comes in with a mysterious parcel tries to get Stanley to pull himself together and come out with her. After she has gone, he moves to the kitchen to wash himself, hiding there and observing the arrival of the two guests, Nathaniel Goldberg and Dermot McCann, who are looking for a particular place in which to do a specific job. These two strangers resemble the two gunmen in *The Dumb Waiter*, particularly in that McCann, the younger of the two, feels that the organization they represent no longer trusts him—with some reason it appears, for he is questioning its orders. He is, after much pressing, answered by Goldberg, in a "quiet, fluent, official tone":

GOLDBERG: The main issue is a singular issue and quite distinct from your previous work. Certain elements, however, might well approximate in points of procedure to some of your other activities. All is dependent on the attitude of our subject. At all events, McCann, I can assure you that the assignment will be carried out and the mission accomplished with no excessive aggravation to you or myself. Satisfied?
McCANN: Sure. Thank you, Nat.[14]

When Meg joins them she insists that it is Stanley's birthday, and Goldberg immediately suggests that they should have a party, though Stanley protests that it is not really his birthday. Stanley seems a little depressed after the strangers have gone upstairs, and to cheer him up Meg gives him the mysterious parcel, his birthday present. It is a toy drum (to replace his piano!), and the first act ends with Stanley marching around the room beating his drum—the beat growing more and more savage until, in the end, he is completely and frighteningly out of control.

Act Two opens with McCann alone, tearing a newspaper into five strips slowly and painstakingly—surely a reasonable dramatization of the insecurity betrayed in Act One.[15] Stanley comes in and tries to find out what Goldberg and McCann have in common, and what associations the two strangers have with his previous life in either Basingstoke or Ireland. He also tries to get rid of them by saying there is no room; and, after a little "game" of sitting down and standing up, he finds himself being questioned in return. McCann and Goldberg begin an interrogation that takes the form of a kind of litany in which serious and frivolous charges are balanced in the syntax of denunciation:

GOLDBERG: Where is your lechery leading you?
McCANN: You'll pay for this.
GOLDBERG: You stuff yourself with dry toast.
McCANN: You contaminate womankind.
GOLDBERG: Why don't you pay the rent?
McCANN: Mother defiler!
GOLDBERG: Why do you pick your nose?
McCANN: I demand justice!
GOLDBERG: What's your trade?
McCANN: What about Ireland?

GOLDBERG:	What's your trade?
STANLEY:	I play the piano.
GOLDBERG:	How many fingers do you use?
STANLEY:	No hands!
GOLDBERG:	No society would touch you. Not even a building society.
McCANN:	You're a traitor to the cloth.
GOLDBERG:	What do you use for pyjamas?
STANLEY:	Nothing.
GOLDBERG:	You verminate the sheet of your birth.
McCANN:	What about the Albigensenist heresy?
GOLDBERG:	Who watered the wicket in Melbourne?
McCANN:	What about the blessed Oliver Plunkett?
GOLDBERG:	Speak up Webber. Why did the chicken cross the road?[16]

The mounting violence and ugliness of this scene is deflected only by the arrival of Meg in her party dress beating Stanley's drum. The party follows, whose central event is a speech by Goldberg (echoing Meg's evocation of her childhood pink room with its night light) in which he regrets the loss of love, which was so comfortably present in those nursery days: "How can I put it to you? We all wander on our tod through this world. It's a lonely pillow to kip on."[17]

At first Stanley will not join in his own party; but when Lulu suggests a game of blindman's buff, he is drawn in. At this point we detect echoes of *The Room;* there is even a song about Reilly. As the blindfolded Stanley picks his way across the room (McCann removes his spectacles first and quietly breaks them), McCann pushes the drum in his way, and Stanley crashes his foot through it. There is great merriment until he catches Meg and tries to strangle her. At this point all the lights go out. In the ensuing melee, McCann drops his flashlight (Goldberg's orders were apparently that Stanley should be kept spotlighted all the time), and, when it is found, Lulu "is lying spreadeagled on the table, Stanley is bent over her." When Goldberg and McCann approach him with the light, he retreats giggling to the wall.

The third act opens once more with breakfast at the Boles's. Meg and Petey (who could not attend the party) discuss both the party and Stanley's illness. His friends are looking after him, and Goldberg's large car waits outside to take him away. Stanley has had some sort of breakdown. Petey offers to help—to get a doctor or to find tape to repair the broken glasses—but such offers are brushed aside by the smoothly professional Goldberg. However, when McCann comes down from Stanley's room, he seems upset and begins to tear the newspaper into strips; but this time rapidly. In the tension of this scene and because

McCann inadvertently calls Goldberg " Simey," a quarrel breaks out.
The fight between Goldberg and McCann is terminated by Goldberg's
statement of faith: never change and always do what you are told:

> Because I believe that the world . . . *(Vacant)*. . . .
> Because I believe that the world . . . *(Desperate)*. . . .
> BECAUSE I BELIEVE THAT THE WORLD . . .
>   *(Lost)*. . . .[18]

This uneasiness also appears to be physical. Goldberg has to have a
kind of medical check-up and the "kiss-of-life" treatment to reassure
himself that he is in perfect condition.

Lulu arrives, and after the events of the last night is surprised to find
that Goldberg is leaving:

LULU: You're leaving?
GOLDBERG: Today.
LULU *(with growing anger)*:   You used me for a night. A passing fancy.
GOLDBERG: Who used who?
LULU: You made use of me by cunning when my defences were
                 down.
GOLDBERG: Who took them down?
LULU: That's what you did. You quenched your ugly thirst. You
                 took advantage of me when I was overwrought. I wouldn't
                 do those things again, not even for a Sultan!
GOLDBERG: One night doesn't make a harem.
LULU: You taught me things a girl shouldn't know before she's been
                 married at least three times!
GOLDBERG: Now you're a jump ahead! What are you complaining
                 about?[19]

The return of McCann, who has gone to get Stanley ready, darkens the
scene and turns this comic game into another potential interrogation,
but when Lulu is ordered to confess, she wisely leaves. Stanley is
brought in transformed: striped trousers, black jacket, white collar, carrying a bowler hat and his broken glasses.[20] He is clean, neat, and
shaven and the two men begin to woo him with relish. But Stanley is
also dumb and their promises only produce a wordless wail. Petey
makes one last attempt to intervene, but on being invited to go along,
he, too, retreats, and the two men take Stanley away to "Monty." The
play closes with Meg still unaware that Stanley has gone, remembering
how she was the belle of the ball.

V   *Criticism of* The Birthday Party

Reviews of *The Birthday Party* were almost unanimously dismissive. Milton Shulman, in the *Evening Standard,* thought the play would be best enjoyed by those who thought obscurity was its own reward; *The Times* found madness in Act One, delirium in Act Two, while the third act "studiously refrains from the slightest hint of what the other two may have been about"; the *Manchester Guardian* advised Pinter to forget Beckett, Ionesco, and Simpson and he might do better next time. The inclusion of Simpson is interesting, particularly as Milton Shulman thought that the play was not nearly as witty as Simpson's *The Resounding Tinkle.* But who, now, remembers N. F. Simpson? Harold Hobson came to the defense of the play in *The Sunday Times* (May 25), claiming that Pinter possessed "the most original, disturbing and arresting talent in theatrical London." He also pointed out that if unfavorable notices do not help the box office (by the time his review appeared the play had closed) their lasting effect is nothing. Pinter was in the best of company—Beckett, Osborne, Shaw, and Ibsen. But, of course, in the theater notices and the box office do matter. Is Pinter going to be encouraged to write more plays? The story of Pinter's development as a dramatist is very much also a story of education of the critics and by the critics. This need for education of audiences was stressed by Irving Wardle in his sympathetic review in *Encore:*

Nowadays there are two ways of saying you don't understand a play: the first is to howl it out with the word "obscurity," once so popular in poetry reviews; the second way is to say that the seminal influence of Ionesco can be detected.

Mr. Pinter received the full treatment. As well as standing for x in the formula above, he was described as inferior to N. F. Simpson, a lagging surrealist, and as the equal of Henry James. Remembering James's melancholy affair with the theater this last one carries a nasty sting; and within a couple of days of receiving it, *The Birthday Party* was over.

But Wardle observed that it was Pinter's "instinct for what will work in the theater that prompted hostility" and he pointed to the example of McCann tearing up strips of paper as a device that introduces a theatrical idea and lets it find its own road back to common sense. There was, moreover, a theme, namely that the man who has withdrawn to protect his illusions will not be helped by being propelled into the outside world. In the protected world a memory or two remain and when the intruders arrive they seem "as much furies emerging from Stanley's night thoughts as physical creatures. His downfall is swift. Scrubbed, shaved, hoisted out of his shapeless trousers, and stuffed into a morning suit he is led away at the end in a catatonic trance."[21]

Six years later *The Birthday Party* was revived in the Aldwych Theatre Summer Repertoire for 1964 with Pinter as director. The critical attention this time was more respectful. There were still, naturally, those who continued to believe that they had been right in 1958. Philip Hope-Wallace, in the *Guardian* (June 19), conceded that "a mild but palpable theatrical excitement is distilled and hangs in the air like an indefinable odor of holiness" while W. A. Darlington, in *The Daily Telegraph* (of the same day), found the play more enjoyable but still wanted to know, exactly, what it was that Stanley had done. For Bamber Gascoigne, in the *Observer* (June 21), Pinter's direction had made the situation too plain and ordinary for characters who were not ordinary, and the second cast failed to produce a gallery of fascinating grotesques in the way the first cast had. This plainness was no real gain since the meaning remained ordinary: "the pressures and guilt brought to bear by ideas of family and success (Goldberg), politics and religion (McCann) on a second-rate artist who has opted out of society and just wants to vegetate."

In fact, this second production, by holding off the horror aspects and allowing itself to be taken as broad comedy (which broadened noticeably as the production got into its stride), left little for the critic to say, as John Russell Taylor whimsically suggested in his review in the August issue of *Plays and Players:* if less than an ideal reading the production was "something unique in the contemporary Theater" and should not be missed. The production had a rightness about it, the sense of which became clearer with reseeing. Because the "explanation" was clearer the menace became all the more unreasonable. Pinter also threw emphasis upon certain aspects the text cannot. Stanley was stronger as a character, bandying words with the strangers, tormenting Meg with the idea of her being carted away in a wheelbarrow which haunts her still at the end of the play. The extremely slow pace of the play gradually justified itself. Thus McCann's irritatingly slow tearing up of the newspaper in Act Two was matched by the swift tearing up in Act Three. The comedy of the opening darkens very slowly, and if we did not feel much sympathy for anyone by the end of the play we

were frightened into recognizing that we could not dismiss our fears
by turning the play into an allegory about the artist in society, that
here was something we might apply, if we dared, to our own lives—a
feeling that matures later in *The Caretaker*, where we recognize that
we all have a Sidcup—and if it is no cosmic Sidcup it is, nevertheless,
frightening and not without eschatalogical implications.

VI   *Some Interpretations of* The Birthday Party

Bert O. States has called the present game "filling Pinter pauses with
O'Neill psychology";[22] we seek to explain our responses and we do so
in terms of allegory and footnotes. Let us take the famous interrogation
in which Goldberg and McCann attack Stanley; in 1962 Bernard
Dukors saw this as part of a general reflection in Pinter's plays of the
tensions and attitudes of an England that was no longer a colonial
power. The plays show man being reduced to a cipher, and his vain
fight against that reduction. Principally rebels must be crushed, and of
these the artist is the chief. In this context Dukors examines the two
henchmen of society who bring the pressure to bear, pointing out that
they represent the two traditional religions of Western civilization,
Judaism and Catholicism (it would be inappropriate to send a
Protestant):

Each has several given names, and these carry connotations of tradition and
religion. McCann is sometimes called Dermot (Diarmaid) and sometimes Sea-
mus (James); Goldberg is called Nat (Nathan) but his wife used to call him
Simey (Simon or Simeon), and his father called him Benjamin (Benny); and
Goldberg has a son named Emmanuel whom he calls Timmy. Their names
change according to the function they perform. For example, although Goldberg's father called him Benny (Benjamin was Jacob's youngest son and the
favorite of his old age), he is in his present capacity called Nat, and just as
Nathan the prophet, commanded directly by God, rebuked King David for
having sinned against the Lord, and brought him back to the paths of right-
eousness, so does Nat, commanded directly by the organization, bring Stanley
back to the paths of conformity. While Goldberg supplies the brains, McCann
supplies the muscle (the Church Militant), and at one point exhorts a young
lady to get down on her knees and confess.[23]

This takes the names very seriously. But if Pinter is using punning
names, what of Boles and Webber? The process is erratic and inex-
haustible. Yet we remember Vivien Merchant's comment that David

was hiding Harold and Vivien was hiding Ada, and that Pinter's agent Emmanuel Wax is always called Jimmy!

The same kind of detail is provided by Stephen Gale on the contents of the interrogation. But surely the name "Oliver Plunkett" was chosen as much for sound as for the fact that he was the last Catholic martyr to die in England? Similarly we are told that Drogheda "was the stronghold first of the Danes and then the Anglo-Normans and the site of several parliaments. In a rebellion in 1641 the town was besieged but relieved, only to fall to Oliver Cromwell in 1649, when the inhabitants were massacred." There follows a list of ruins in the vicinity. We almost expect a note directing us to Chapter 13 of *Oliver Cromwell* by Antonia Fraser! Does Pinter work like this? Not according to Quigley, who comments, rather clumsily:

Their function is to overcome Stanley by the quantity of accusation not by the truth-quality of any particular accusation. Here again the language is primarily used in the negotiation of the relationship between Stanley and his visitors rather than for its overall referential possibilities. If anything, the diversity of potential referential usage is subordinated to and organized by an interrelational motive and goal.[24]

In calling the interrogation a litany I was trying to pin down a halfway house between these viewpoints. The details are meaningful but blurred by repetition; but repetition suggests practice. Goldberg and McCann perform the ritual like professionals, they have done it before and they make a great team. But they are frightening also because they exhibit doubt and fear—when Petey opens his newspaper at the end of the play five carefully torn strips flutter out, reminding us how ill at ease Goldberg and McCann have been. It is true that Pinter in his poem on the play, "A View of the Party" (it is *a* view not *the* view), does suggest that Goldberg is the center of the play and might be more than an agent of the power. The second part of the poem also hints that they are essentially forces in the mind of Stanley, but if so they are embodied furies. They promise Stanley a new birth:

GOLDBERG: We'll make a man of you.
McCANN: And a woman.
GOLDBERG: You'll be reoriented.
McCANN: You'll be rich.
GOLDBERG: You'll be adjusted.
McCANN: You'll be our pride and joy.

GOLDBERG: You'll be a mensch.
McCANN: You'll be a success.
GOLDBERG: You'll be integrated.
McCANN: You'll give orders.
GOLDBERG: You'll make decisions.[25]

Of course Meg has invented the birthday because she wants to give Stanley a present: the drum. A present, friends, a party—even if rape, attempted murder, and a nervous breakdown ensue—are suggestive, as is the play's title, of coziness. R. F. Storch claims that the menace comes precisely from family feelings "served up in a heavy syrup of sentimentality":

McCann's version is of course the familiar Irish kind (James Joyce's young man had to escape from it too, though it continued to haunt him). Goldberg and McCann make a team—enterprising, loyal, and doing a job. Not necessarily a criminal job. The point is that any job done in this team spirit becomes sinister. . . . The team spirit belongs to the same world as family sentiment: both reach out their tentacles to strangle Stanley.[26]

This is possibly an American viewpoint (though the British public school springs to mind as an equivalent) and is certainly a more indigenous interpretation than comparison with Kafka. It is true that in *The Trial* the hero has guilt feelings and is taken away to be executed by two respectable-looking gentlemen. To a Polish critic like Gregorz Sinko Kafka is the obvious key: "One feels like saying that the two executioners, Goldberg and McCann, stand for all the principles of state and social conformism. Goldberg refers to his 'job' in a typically Kafkaesque official language which deprives the crime of all sense and reality." As for his removal at the end of the play: "Maybe Stanley will meet his death there or maybe he will only receive a conformist brainwashing after which he is promised . . . many other gifts of civilization. . . ."[27] This may be appropriate to a Polish reader for whom the world of Kafka is not entirely fictional but in the context of an English seaside resort? Such a context suggests Graham Greene's *Brighton Rock* and the contrast between the vicious adult world and the safe night-lighted world of childhood recalls Greeneland—seediness, professional thugs, and traitors. And Kafka and Greene must coexist with another layer since Meg's illusions as belle of the ball are reminiscent of, say, Tennessee Williams. It is the number of layers that fascinates even if they may not have been too perfectly molded together:

simultaneously we have "an allegory about the rise of fascism, a seaside social comedy, and a sexual farce."[28] What is interesting about the "allegory" is the reversal of racial sterotypes: here the Jew and the Irishman become instruments of vengeance on the Englishman! We may find it hard to accept Baker/Tabachnik's contention that Stanley's special treatment is probably circumcision but their interpretation of the play as being about Pinter, the assimilated Jewish artist with feelings of guilt over his betrayal of the group, is plausible. Goldberg's fury when he is called Simey occurs because the name gives him away and disturbs his harmony with the Christian world:

Goldberg flees from his position as a marginal man, a Jew in a Christian world, into an ethnic past of family, food and Fridays that may never have existed for him particularly. Such happy reminiscence of the past becomes a Pinter medium in later plays. . . . But the past offers Goldberg no escape, although he progressively retreats into it as the play moves. . . . At best it affords him some communication at the universal level with the equally maudlin memories of the other characters.[29]

This interpretation, then, sees Stanley turned into a renegade Jew just as McCann accuses him of the same crime in Irish terms, betrayal of the IRA. Stanley accepts the role and acts out on Meg and Lulu the sex and violence of which he stands accused. Such pressures only reappear so intensely again in *The Homecoming*. The party is, of course, a Bar Mitzvah (which means "Son of Duty"), the ritual that marks the age of responsibility, of Stanley's becoming a man.

What Stanley's crime or punishment is we simply do not know, nor do we need to: our critics are all more or less plausible:

Something for everyone, in fact: somewhere, the author seems to be telling his audience, you have done something—think hard and you may remember what it is—which will one day catch you out. The next time you answer a door to an innocent-looking stranger. . . .[30]

VII   The Dumb Waiter

Although written in 1957, *The Dumb Waiter* was not produced until 1959, and then in Germany. Its first English production was at the Hempstead Theatre Club and later at the Royal Court, in 1960. It takes as its subject the two agents in *The Birthday Party*, or their counterparts, and explores the predicament of the victimizers, not the victim, who while menacing others can themselves be menaced. As Sinko puts it:

When the functionary begins to reflect on the meaning of his job, he must die. The mechanism is a self-regulating one, hence the appropriateness of the ambiguous meaning of the Polish title: Samoobsluga, Self-service. Whatever one might think, the job has to go on. Just as in *The Birthday Party* we have not come close to the secret Court or the Authority living in the castle or at the top of the lift: we have just seen it work from another side.

This play explores the uneasiness expressed by a questioning McCann and a faltering Goldberg. *The Dumb Waiter* is a genuine comedy of menace set in a basement in Birmingham and in it Pinter begins to use silence as part of the dialogue, playing off a loquacious character against a silent one. Gus cannot bear silence and Ben resents talk.

The basement room has no windows and only one door leading out into the unknown; the other door opens into a defective lavatory. Here, two men of no particular age, called Ben and Gus, are waiting. Ben has a newspaper from which he occasionally reads out diverting passages and from behind which he watches irritably as Gus moves restlessly about the room or makes frequent visits to the faulty toilet. Their rambling conversation is about trivial matters—items in the newspapers, the crockery they have been provided with, who is playing whom at football next Saturday—trivia interrupted by questions from Gus about the length of the job they are on and what time "he" is likely to get in touch with them. Ben resents this kind of question, excessively, it seems, just as Gus's annoyance with the room seems excessive. Gus likes to have "a bit of a view." Ben, with his woodwork and model boats, replies that Gus ought to have a hobby, though its usefulness in the present situation hardly seems pressing. Gus goes on asking questions. Why, for example, did Ben stop the car early that morning when he thought Gus was asleep? These occasional remarks, running through the ordinary conversation on football and everyday events, combine with the tension that obviously exists between Ben and Gus, and gradually build up a sense of something sinister behind the casual presence of two men waiting to do a job in Birmingham.

When an envelope containing twelve matches is pushed under the door and a revolver is snatched from under a pillow, we become more and more certain that these cannot be ordinary working men, that their job is no everyday job, that, in fact, they are two hired assassins, part of a large and mysterious organization, and that their occupation is traveling up and down the country killing people to order. Thus the seemingly trivial argument over the phrase "light a kettle" is more than a semantic quibble. It summarizes the relative positions of the two men, and when Ben, wearily, forgets and says, "Put on the bloody kettle," the inadequacy of his position of not asking questions is revealed. Such arguments lay a comic foundation for the main question of the play. Moreover, Gus's irritation over smelly sheets, crockery that is not so good as it has been, not having a window, and being permanently on call are really symptoms of his disquiet about the job itself:

GUS.   I was just thinking about that girl, that's all. (GUS *sits on his bed.*) She wasn't much to look at, I know, but still. It was a mess though, wasn't it? What a mess. Honest, I can't remember a mess like that one. They don't seem to hold together like men, women. A looser texture, like. Didn't she spread, eh? She didn't half spread. Kaw! But I've been meaning to ask you. (BEN *sits up and clenches his eyes.*) Who clears up after we've gone? I'm curious about that. Who does the clearing up? Maybe they don't clear up. Maybe they just leave them there, eh? What do you think? How many jobs have we done? Blimey, I can't count them. What if they never clear anything up after we've gone.

BEN   *(Pityingly):*   You mutt. Do you think we're the only branch of this organization? Have a bit of common. They got departments for everything.

GUS: What cleaners and all?

BEN: You birk!

GUS: No, it was that girl made me start to think. . . .[31]

Further thought, however, is prevented by a clatter from the back of the room, where there is, after all, another entrance to this room: a serving hatch or dumb waiter, which suddenly starts to descend with orders on it for food. The gunmen, anxious not to be discovered, try to fulfill those orders with what food they have brought with them: an Eccles cake, a bar of chocolate, half a pint of milk, and a packet of potato chips. When Ben accuses Gus of hiding the one Eccles cake from him, it is, in view of the end of the play, a rather ironic reproach. But we could explain a great deal of edginess on Ben's part because he knows or suspects what he will have to do. The knowledge that he will have to get rid of his mate could account for his resentment at the beginning of the play and subsequently.

The orders for food continue to arrive, becoming more and more exotic, from macaroni pastitsio and ormitha macarounda to scampi. The two men shout up the serving hatch that they have sent everything up. Since this has no effect, they decide to send a written message. At this point, they notice a speaking tube, but it will only work for Ben, who speaks into it with great deference and is told something. Ben and Gus then rehearse the killing in a duologue that, significantly, leaves out the order for Gus to take out his gun. After this, the two men return to the newspaper game, but on a more muted level. While Gus is once more in the defective lavatory, Ben gets his orders—to shoot the next person to come in—and when Gus enters through the door, Ben is facing him, gun in hand, and, presumably, shoots him at the end of the slow curtain.

The main element of comedy is provided by the dialogue—talk to pass the time while Ben and Gus wait, not for Godot, but for orders. Their moral indignation over items in the newspaper (about a man of eighty-seven who crawled under a truck and was run over or the child of eight who killed a cat) contrasts with their own job; it also implies that they are just doing a job, like any other job; and, as long as they regard it as that, they are adequate gunmen. The discussions on football, making tea, and what to do on Saturday become terrifying when we see what these men are. But Gus is no longer a good gunman; he has begun to think about the victims and question the orders and efficiency of the organization. We suspect that the orders from above will lead to tragedy, but this tragedy clearly satisfies the postulate of Ionesco that tragedy should always be fused with hilarious farce. The play is much more comic than either of the preceding plays, though there is, presumably, a victim. The play is about the difference between Ben (the dumb waiter) and Gus (who by asking questions is rebelling). Whereas Ben accepts orders and is an almost perfect cog in the larger machine, Gus is becoming an individual and must be eliminated. Ironically, this very elimination might in turn unsettle Ben, who might, in turn, have to be eliminated also.

VIII   Critical Interpretations

The end of the play is open, a device that Pinter is to use frequently in later plays. We assume that Gus will be shot and this assumption confirms the serious element of the play. But it is a very comic play, too. The sight of two serious gunmen trying to answer heavenly

demands for exotic food is hilarious, and possibly this larger comic element has suggested that the piece is slight. It is certainly less "symbolic" than, say, its companion one-act play, *The Room*. Critics have
complained that it has the air of a dramatized anecdote, but it is not
without significance even as a footnote to *The Birthday Party*. There
the "team spirit" was sinister. Martin Esslin asks whether the army
(which Pinter so strenuously refused to join) is very different to the
organization that sends out Gus and Ben; both require obedience and
killing. Dumb obviously means mute, but it may also indicate a certain
lack of intelligence, or sensitivity to the job in hand:

This picture of a job for everyone and everything, with everyone performing
his own speciality is close enough to a description of modern society for the
correlation to be drawn. Here, then, the play becomes a depiction of the fate
of a sensitive man . . . presenting a threat to society because he questions
rather than accepts, and who must therefore be destroyed before he
destroys.[32]

But we must not overload the play with significance; suggestions about
the twelve matches (the Apostles?) and a Trinity of gas rings on the
stove are surely far-fetched. J. W. Lambert's introduction to the play
in the Penquin edition sums up the play admirably:

This glimpse of two hired killers is told not merely without heightened prose
but in the lowest common denominator of human speech—a dialogue in
which every phrase is drawn straight from life at a level of intellectual
vacancy which might seem the death of drama; but which is handled with
such a sure command of pause and repetition that evokes simultaneously the
laughter of contemptuous recognition and a shiver of dread. As within ourselves, on the one hand open up abysses of bottomless inanity, and the other
loom the fearful crags of an irrational, implacable cruelty.
   Bizarre and claustrophobic as it is, Mr. Pinter's exploration of the lower
depths has an unmistakeable, if indefinable relevance to life as we live it. But
it is not, of course, explicitly sociological.[33]

IX   A Slight Ache *and Other Plays*

Besides these three stage plays, Pinter's early work includes plays for
the radio and revue sketches: *A Slight Ache* (1959), broadcast by the
BBC; sketches for two revues; and two plays for radio, *A Night Out*
(completed in 1959 and broadcast in 1960) and *The Dwarfs*, broadcast

by the BBC Third Program, also in 1960. In these works Pinter explored his techniques and themes but also shifted the tone of his treatment.

A *Slight Ache* is a play for which Pinter has a very great affection. Written in the post–*Birthday Party* period of failure it established, for him, the right to write as he pleased. Its setting is different: a country house with a garden. If the opening scene between Edward and Flora at breakfast reminds us of *The Room* and *The Birthday Party*, Edward and Flora are obviously from a different social class, they are more articulate, and their room opens out on to a large garden. It is this garden and its plants which is the subject of the argument that opens the play and which is crystallized by the arrival of a wasp which Edward kills with great satisfaction by trapping it in the marmalade pot and pouring boiling water on it.

Once the wasp has been despatched Edward begins to reveal what his real worry is, a matchseller who has been standing at the back gate for two months. Both Edward and Flora use the word "bullock" to describe him, and in some way, he is a catalyst for the inadequacy of the relationship between Edward and Flora. Thus, when Flora calls her husband "Beddie Weddie," Edward's annoyance is surely only partly because she is treating him as a baby. Finally, Edward insists that Flora invite the matchseller in; and the rather revolting but totally silent creature becomes the focus of the histories of both characters. From these histories, which may or may not be true, the play builds up on the antagonisms between Edward and Flora—the inadequacy of Edward and the desires of Flora (her Laurentian rape speech is so elegantly told it must be fantasy).

Edward begins to emerge as the more significant character because he is asking questions. To ask questions is always dangerous, as we have seen in *The Dumb Waiter*, and here questioning the appearance, motives, or implications of the matchseller invites disaster. For Flora the matchseller is no problem—she gives him a name, Barnabas (son of exhortation), and in naming him solves the problem of his identity. Barnabas becomes, for her, the desirable combination of child, husband, and lover that the apparently dominant Edward never could be. Edward, however, begins to show what is behind his bullying, self-sufficient facade. Pinter gives him two long speeches. His first speech is a history, as is Flora's long speech; but the second one is less a history and more a probe in which he tries to define the matchseller, put a name on him, and put him into a context which is comprehensible. He uses such questions and statements as what game do you play, or, you remind me of Cavendish. He contrasts this lack of definition with yesterday's clarity:

Yesterday, now it was clear, clearly defined, so clearly.
(Pause.)
The garden, too, was sharp, lucid, in the rain, in the sun.
(Pause.)
My den, too, was sharp, arranged for my purpose . . . quite satisfactory.
(Pause.)
The house, too, was polished, all the bannisters were polished, and the stair rods, and the curtain rods.
(Pause.)
My desk was polished, and my cabinet.
(Pause.)
I was polished. *(Nostalgic.)* . . .[34]

Now all this brightness and clarity merely dazzles Edward into blindness. At this point the opening argument over the names of flowers becomes more understandable. So does the significance of Flora's last entrance, when she offers Barnabas an orderly polished house: her husband has been reduced to the silence of the matchseller (just as Rose became blind and Stanley dumb). Edward asks questions in search of information, but when Barnabas says nothing, Edward is obliged to invent questions for him. Before this silence, his crisp English middle-class reticence crumbles and he moves into an orgy of confession and self-examination that is concerned, from the beginning, with the basic question, who or what *is* the matchseller? Desperately, Edward tries to pin him down: for over two months he has looked at the matchseller in all weathers from all angles and in all lights. The examination breaks down the examiner—there is no answer to the question, who are you? The play ends with the substitution of Edward for the matchseller.

Basically, there are the usual properties in *A Slight Ache:* a room, uneasy inhabitants, and an intruder who will destroy the precarious if unhappy coziness. But here the "threat" is more completely located inside the characters; indeed, a radio audience could not verify whether or not the matchseller really exists outside the imagination of Edward and Flora. Gale feels this is an irrelevance since he does exist in the stage version and anyway the other two characters act as if he does exist, but this indecisiveness does help to point to the true source of the action: the unfulfilled needs of the man and the woman—psychological rather than physical menace. Trussler has objected that the play suffers badly "from never being about a middle-class couple and a matchseller. It is all symbol and no substance, with quite a few footnotes thrown in to make up the weight."[35] John Russell Brown, on the other hand, finds it Pinter's simplest play! It must be remembered that as a radio play the language has to carry all the weight of the action; and this at least illustrates Pinter's ability to write dialogue outside the vernacular of low life, to capture the class differences that still matter so much in English life and which, as Shaw observed in *Pygmalion*, are frequently a matter of how we speak.

Here Pinter's room has a window and a view (anticipating *The Lover* in theme and setting) and the menace is invited in for examination and plays a completely passive role, to become, in fact, no more than the object in relation to which Edward and Flora act out their fantasies and inadequacies. The venom of the action suggests that the inadequacies are sexual, though whether we feel it as a version of the *Bacchae*, as Burkman suggests, in which Flora, the earth mother, sacrifices the old god for the new is another matter. She is certainly the central character, because whether earth goddess or not she is the one in motion taking on the new role as wife and mother; whereas Edward breaks down when confronted with the silence of the matchseller, a subject explored in the short story written in 1955, "The Examination," and developed still further in another short story, "Tea Party."[36]

X   *"The Examination"*

This short story, first published in the summer 1959 issue of *Prospect* (reprinted with *The Lover* and *The Collection* in 1963), is, obviously, not an academic examination in spite of the presence of chalk and a blackboard. It could be compared with the interview sketch "Applicant" and it recalls the prose poem "Kullus": it involves the situation basic to *A Slight Ache* and *The Basement*. The story contains three favorite motifs: a room, domination, and silence. In the examination of Kullus by the Examiner (the "I" of the story) we watch a gradual shift of the dominant to the dominated, which was the theme that attracted Pinter to the film of *The Servant:*

That short story dealt very explicitly with two people in one room having a battle of an unspecified nature, in which the question was one of who was dominant at what point and how they were going to be dominant and what tools they would use to achieve dominance and how they would try to undermine the other person's dominance. A threat is constantly there; it's got to do with this question of being in the uppermost position, or attempting to be. That's something of what attracted me to do the screenplay of *The Servant*, which was someone else's story you know. I wouldn't call this violence so much as a battle for positions, it's a very common everyday thing.[37]

Of course, in the film, Pinter has the advantage of class warfare and sex; Kullus's sole weapon here seems to be his silence:

When Kullus was disposed to silence I invariably acquiesced, and prided myself on those occasions with tactical acumen. But I did not regard these silences as intervals, for they were not, and neither, I think, did Kullus so regard them. For if Kullus fell silent, he did not cease to participate in our examination. Never, at any time, had I reason to doubt his active participation, through word and through silence, between interval and interval, and I recognised what I took to be his devotion as actual and unequivocal, besides, as it seemed to me, obligatory. And so the nature of our silence within the frame of our examination, and the nature of our silence outside the frame of our examination, were entirely opposed.

The difference between the two characters is also illustrated, as in *The Basement*, by differences in their rooms; by the end of the story Kullus has not merely noticed the differences between his room and that of the Examiner, he has removed them. The Examiner does not object. He continues, however, to try to understand the nature of Kullus's silences, and his anxiety to do so leads him finally to accept his own Examination by Kullus. By the end he has changed places and rooms with Kullus.

The language in this story is reminiscent of the philosophical content of *The Dwarfs* and later *The Homecoming* as well as *A Slight Ache*. It must be remembered, however, that both *A Slight Ache* and *The Dwarfs* were written for radio, plays that gave scope (too much, perhaps) to Pinter the poet. *A Slight Ache* also marks the end of Pinter's first period, one of relative obscurity. It was commissioned by the BBC Third Program, which serves a minority audience; *The Dumb Waiter* was first produced in Germany; and neither *The Room* nor *The Birthday Party* had been particularly successful. Henceforth audiences and critical approval will grow, and the description "Comedies of Menace" ceases to be useful.

XI *Revue Sketches*

Writing these revue sketches not only helped Pinter financially, but they also helped him to perfect the comic side of his art, although all of them are tinged with sadness, the pathetic, or the sinister. Pinter has not published two of them, "Special Offer" and "Getting Acquainted"; indeed, the latter, apparently a farcical episode built round a civil defense practice, is, according to him, lost. The former, however, is a brief account of a BBC lady disturbed by a special offer in a leading London store which Mr. Pinter has allowed to be printed here:

SECRETARY *(at desk in office)*: Yes, I was in the rest room at Swan and Edgars, having a little rest. Just sitting there, interfering with nobody, when this old crone suddenly came right up to me and sat beside me. You're on the staff of the B.B.C. she said, aren't you? As a matter of fact I am, I said. What can I do for you? I've got just the thing for you, she said, and put a little card into my hand. Do you know what was written on it? MEN FOR SALE! What on earth do you mean? I said. Men, she said, all sorts shapes and sizes, for sale. What on earth can you *possibly mean?* I said. It's an international congress, she said, got up for the entertainment and relief of lady members of the civil service. You can hear some of the boys we've got speak through a microphone, especially for your pleasure, singing little folk tunes we're sure you've never heard before. Tea is on the house and every day we have the very best pastries. For the cabaret at teatime the boys do a rare dance imported all the way from Buenos Aires, dressed in nothing but a pair of cricket pads. Every single one of them is tried and tested, very best quality, and at very reasonable rates. If you like one of them by any of his individual characteristics you can buy him, but for you not at retail price. As you work for the B.B.C. we'll be glad to make a special reduction. If you're at all dissatisfied you can send him back within seven days and have your money refunded. That's *very* kind of you, I said, but as a matter of fact I've just been on leave, I start work tomorrow and am perfectly refreshed. And I left her where she was. Men for Sale! What an extraordinary idea! I've never heard of anything so outrageous, have you? Look—here's the card.
(Pause)
Do you think it's a joke . . . or serious?

An extraordinary idea indeed; but what's sauce for the goose ought, perhaps, to be sauce for the gander. Implicit in this slight sketch is precisely the reversal of roles that audiences found so shocking in *The Homecoming*.

Two of the sketches in print are about interviews: "Trouble in the

Works" and "Applicant." The first grew out of a job that Pinter held
for half a day in a factory service department where he had to copy
down the names of machine parts. It is a skit on terminology in heavy
engineering with splendid sexual overtones. A works manager receives
complaints from the workers' representative about certain objects they
are making and to which they have taken a dislike:

WILLS: They've just taken a turn against the whole lot of them, I tell you.
         Male elbow adaptors, tubing nuts, grub screws, internal fan wash-
         ers, dog points, half dog points, white metal bushes—
FIBBS: But not, surely, my lovely parallel male stud couplings?
WILLS: They hate and detest your lovely parallel male stud couplings, and
         the straight flange pump connectors, and back nuts, and front nuts,
         and the bronze draw off cock with handwheel and the bronze
         draw off cock without handwheel![38]

When Fibbs asks, despairingly, what the men do want to make, the
answer is brisk and to the point: Brandy Balls. This, for some curious
reason, was changed, in the NBC television production "Pinter People," to Love.

"Applicant" apparently comes from the unpublished *The Hothouse*
(q.v.) and concerns the fate of an applicant for a job who is fitted with
electrodes and bombarded with impossible questions (for example: Are
you virgo intacta? Have you always been virgo intacta?) until he suffers a complete collapse, a situation halfway between the interrogations
in *The Birghday Party* and the shock treatment in *The Caretaker*. The
other three sketches show two or more characters allowed to interact:
"The Black and White" (two old tramp women compare notes on how
to pass the night), "Last to Go" (a newspaper seller and the proprietor
of a coffee stall discuss which paper is the last to be sold),[39] and
"Request Stop" (a slightly mad woman pesters a man at a bus stop with
a question and then insists, loudly, that he has made an improper suggestion to her).

XII   A Night Out

This radio play was almost immediately transferred to television,
where it had a record audience of between 15 and 18 million viewers.
Like the revue sketches it is a simple play. Pinter felt there was no real
difference between sketch and play: "In both I am interested primarily

in people: I want to present living people to the audience, worthy of
their interest primarily because they *are*, they exist, not because of any
moral the author may draw from them."[40]

Looking at *A Night Out* it is tempting to see Pinter as moving
toward a greater realism, but, in fact, the menacers in *The Birthday
Party* belong to the normal world and behave more like ordinary people than not, while the gunmen in *The Dumb Waiter* are shown as
ordinary people with an extraordinary job; in both plays violence has
been toned down. If we exclude the wasp episode violence in the physical sense has also been excluded from *A Slight Ache*, a trend that
continues in *The Caretaker*, where menace is a practical joke; it is
obviously a clash of personalities that causes displacement. *A Night
Out* occurs within a varied and normal context, contains no symbols or
any mystery, though Esslin, rather oddly, insists that it ends on a question: is he free? It shows the new directness and simplicity we see in
Night School (Chapter 5) and *The Caretaker* (Chapter 4). Esslin's view
of the ending is odd because though the title does suggest a note of
defiance it also confirms that this is a rare if not unique occasion: Albert
breaks out of his room, but room service is soon restored.

The play opens with Albert Stokes trying to escape from a possessive
mother who will not admit that her husband is dead or that grandma
has been dead for ten years—will not admit these facts linguistically,
at any rate—and whose principal worry is that Albert will grow up
and leave her for another girl:

MOTHER *(following)*: Albert.
ALBERT: What?
MOTHER: I want to ask you a question.
ALBERT: What?
MOTHER: Are you leading a clean life?
ALBERT: A clean life?
MOTHER: You're not leading an unclean life, are you?
ALBERT: What are you talking about?
MOTHER: You're not messing about with girls, are you? You're not going
           to go messing about with girls tonight?
ALBERT: Don't be so ridiculous.
MOTHER: Answer me, Albert. I'm your mother.
ALBERT: I don't know any girls.
MOTHER: If you're going to the firm's party, there'll be girls there, won't
           there? Girls from the office?
ALBERT: I don't like them, any of them.

MOTHER: You promise?
ALBERT: Promise what?
MOTHER: That . . . that you won't upset your father.
ALBERT: My father? How can I upset my father? You're always talking about upsetting people who are dead!
MOTHER: Oh, Albert, you don't know how you hurt me, you don't know the hurtful way you've got, speaking of your poor father like that.
ALBERT: But he is dead.
MOTHER: He's not. He's living! *(Touching her breast)* In here! And this is his house![41]

The scene shifts to a coffee stall where two of Albert's colleagues from the office, Seeley and Kedge (the former played by Pinter), are talking about Albert's recent depression, which is spoiling his game of football. At this point, Pinter shifts to a short scene that shows Albert escaping from his mother. He comes to the coffee stall, where his colleagues tease him about a girl (who, they say, is attracted to Albert), his poor game of football, and his mother. The final shot of the act shows the mother laying out a game of patience, the clock ticking on the mantelpiece.

The second act shows the firm's party to say good-bye to an old and trusted member of the company, Mr. Ryan. Here another colleague asks his girl friend's friend, Eileen, to pretend to be friendly with Albert for a joke. Eileen agrees. During the formal speech of farewell, however, Eileen lets out a scream, claims that she has been interfered with, and Albert is blamed. When the firm's accountant, Sidney, taunts Albert with being a mother's boy, Albert hits him and leaves the party. In the television production it was made quite clear that the man who pinched Eileen was old, trusty Mr. Ryan. On the radio such identification was, of course, not possible. The second scene shows Albert's mother asleep in a disorder of playing cards, the clock at twelve, and Albert creeping in. She immediately wakes up and, seeing his disheveled appearance, assumes that he has been messing about with girls. She launches into a long speech on his wickedness in which leaving her alone to go and mess about with girls is confused with leaving his dinner uneaten. Albert breaks down and the act ends when he raises the clock above her head as if he were going to hit her with it.

Act Three shows Albert back at the coffee stall, which is now closed, where he meets a tart who takes him back to her flat. There she insists that she is really a lady of refinement with a daughter attending a select boarding school in Hereford. She complains when Albert swears, insists that he take off his shoes, use the ashtray, and show other marks of respect, or domesticity. Albert retaliates by pretending to be an assistant director in films, which stimulates the girl to reveal her own longing for the violent, sexual, glamorous life she thinks he must lead as a film director. Albert, ignoring this rambling monologue, suddenly picks up the clock. Alarmed, the girl starts to psychoanalyze him, but he deliberately stubs a cigarette out on the carpet, threatens her with the clock, breaks the photograph of the daughter, exposing it as a lie, and, having made her put his shoes on for him, leaves, casually throwing her half a crown. The final scene shows his return to mother, who welcomes him back:

Listen, Albert, I'll tell you what I'm going to do. I'm going to forget it. You see? I'm going to forget all about it. We'll have your holiday in a fortnight. We can go away. *She strokes his hand.* It's not as if you're a bad boy . . . you're a good boy . . . I know you are . . . it's not as if you're really bad, Albert, you're not . . . you're not bad, you're good . . . you're not a bad boy, Albert, I know you're not. . . .
(Pause)
You're good, You're not bad, you're a good boy . . . I know you are . . . you are, aren't you?[42]

Unfortunately for Albert, she is right: the night out is over.

There is really no ambiguity or mystery in the play; the dreams of the tart and Albert are only dreams, the photograph is identified by the inscription on the back, and even the person who interfered with Eileen is identified. The play does bring together the multiple possibility of a woman: mother, girl friend, and tart—but this is not explored; indeed it is deliberately excluded from the next play, *The Dwarfs.* Basically the play is about the relationship between a mother and her son, almost a documented case history of an Oedipus complex;[43] and widening out from that situation the need for lonely or insecure people to have illusions: the *need* to lie. Albert and his mother remind us of the Stanley/Meg situation, but since Albert has not chosen it he resents it; and he is too inadequate to be able, as Stanley can, to turn his mother's stupidity to his own advantage. He feels guilty about going to the party, and so the party is bound to be disastrous. Even when he resorts to violence he has to be content with what Taylor calls "a substitute victory" against a substitute victim—he reproaches the girl, for example, for endless talking, as he does his mother. The mother's willingness to forget and the fact that she remains unharmed at the end of the play suggest that nothing that Albert can do now really matters.

XIII   The Dwarfs

Finally, in 1960, the BBC Third Program broadcast Pinter's play *The Dwarfs*, which was subsequently staged, with Pinter directing, at the New Arts Theatre in September 1963. Of this play Taylor comments that it is the most difficult and daunting to popular taste,[44] while Wellwarth concludes that it was impossible to make anything definite of it.[45] The reactions of the critics and audiences in 1963, in spite of a very sensitive performance by John Hurt in the main part, support these judgments. It is a very private play, written for the radio, a medium that allowed Pinter freedom to experiment and to take risks with words. Thus *The Dwarfs* was an extremely valuable play for Pinter, although he admits that it may have been incomprehensible to the audience.[46]

The play is based on an unpublished novel written sometime between 1950–56, with four characters, three men and a girl called Virginia. In the play only the three men appear, Len, Pete, and Mark. The novel was, apparently, partly autobiographical, about growing up in the East End of London. Len and Mark were Jewish while Pete was not; and Mark was also an actor with Portuguese ancestors. Written over too long a period, in too many styles, and possibly showing too many signs of enthusiasm for Beckett's *Watt*, the only things Pinter felt worth exploring were used in the radio play.[47]

XIV   *The Action of the Play*

The play opens with two typical Pinter characters, Pete and Len, who are waiting in Mark's flat for his return. Initially they remind us a little of Gus and Ben because of their desultory conversation (mainly about food and Mark), and particularly because of Len's incessant questions and Pete's irritation at them. We learn nothing about Pete, but we do gather that Len has a casual job as a porter at Euston station and prefers night work. The excitable nature of Len's interest in things justifies Pete's early remark, "You'll be ready for the looney bin next week if you go on like this." Pete, in contrast, is thoroughly noncommittal; even when Len examines his palm and pronounces Pete a homicidal maniac, he remains unperturbed.

The arrival of Mark ends this scene and the next takes place in Len's room. The text does not prescribe a particular room but the production showed that Len's room was old, inherited from the family, and reminiscent of Edgar Allan Poe in furnishing and decor. Here Len tries to establish his existence by defining, in a manner reminiscent of Ionesco's language-primer dialogue, his table, his chair, his bowl of fruit, and so on.[48] Against this fixed existence, which makes all "clear and abundant" but which is also a "manacle," runs the idea that the room moves (ironically, "to a dead halt"!). At the moment all is ordered, in its place; and Len is wedged: "There are no voices. They make a hole in my side." Since *The Dwarfs* is a play for voices and is certainly "poetic," the hole-in-the-side image could have a religious significance—it is repeated later—but it does not make Len a Christ figure. It reminds us of certain connections, just as Wellwarth may be suggestive in seeing Mark as a papal symbol.[49]

The soliloquy is interrupted by the arrival of Mark in a new suit described (or defined?) in a music-hall patter played out between Len and Mark. Once more the talk is desultory, but behind it is a desire to put a label or price on everything—a desire that holds together statements like "There is a time and place for everything" and "The price of butter is going up."[50] But Mark's presence in the room constitutes a challenge: Len insists that he wants no curiosity there. Since curiosity is a mark of ·the Pinter victim and liberally displayed by Len and rarely, if ever, by Mark, this statement is both ironic and self-commentary. It leads into Len's second statement about the room. In his first description, while conceding mobility (the room rearranges itself if one stops watching it), he emphasizes the quality of "fixture"—albeit an imprisoning one. Len now stresses "mobility" or change. One cannot, he asserts, rely on the natural behavior of a room, however much one wants to. He uses the analogy of sitting in a railway compartment to show unknowability. From his window he can see lights moving that he knows are still and move only because he moves; or rather because he is still but being moved. Only when moving can he know objects, yet only objects in stillness can be known. This is a complicated way of saying that what we think we know can be false, and in the following scene, Pete suggests putting the troublesome furniture in a boat and parking it (that is, not moving it!). Pete delivers a lecture to Len summed up in the line, "Giving up the ghost isn't so much a failure as a tactical error."

Pete insists that Len pull himself together, or he will be locked up. When Len protests that things change every minute, Pete replies that he should discriminate:

You've got no idea how to preserve a distance between what you smell and what you think about it. You haven't got the faculty for making a simple distinction between one thing and another. Every time you walk out of this door you go straight over a cliff. What you've got to do is nourish the power of assessment. How can you hope to assess and verify anything if you walk about with your nose stuck between your feet all day long?[51]

Pete then warns Len that Mark is no good for him and follows this with an account of a strange dream: of himself, in a subway station in which everybody's face was peeling off, rotting and blistering—which reduces Len to groans. It is possible that Pete's nightmare, deliberately thrust on the unstable Len, acts like Goldberg's speeches on Stanley. If, in fact, Pete and Mark are another form of menacers, their powers are ironically extended to the dwarfs themselves. Who or what the dwarfs are, we are not told; they simply organize, carry out a job of some sort, and leave (like fantastic Goldbergs and McCanns?). They are skilled laborers, and their trade is not without risk. Thus they might be phantasmal representatives of the organization that employs Ben and Gus or Goldberg and McCann. We know that in some way Len's standing with them depends on Pete and Mark.

In the next scene, Len, possibly influenced by Pete's dream, asks Mark about his face, and Mark warns Len that Pete is no good for him. Len interrupts this to state once more the close involvement of Len, Pete, Mark, and the dwarfs, using the conjugated verb "he sits, I sit; they stand, I squat." As the dialogue becomes more and more interior, the play seems to consist of a steady progression into Len's private world. Often scenes with Pete and Mark seem more presented by Len than directly experienced by us. The dwarfs, according to Len, have gone off on a picnic, leaving him to clean up their garbage. In another soliloquy he visualizes his two friends as seagull and spider:

Pete walks by the—gull. Slicing gull. Gull. Down. He stops. Stone. Watches. Rat corpse in the yellow grass. Gull pads. Gull probes. Gull stamps his feet. Gull whinnies up. Gull screams, tears, Pete tears, digs, Pete cuts, breaks, Pete stretches the corpse, flaps his wings, Pete's beak grows, probes, digs, pulls, the river jolts, no moon, what can I see. . . .

Mark lies, heavy, content, watches his smoke in the window, times his puff out, his hand fall, *(with growing disgust)* smiles at absent guests, sucks in all comers, arranges his web, lies there a spider.[52]

In a later conversation with Mark, Len tries to question him, but has as little success as with Pete. Important questions like "Do you believe in God?" are bypassed until Len forces the point:

The point is, who are you. Not why or how, not even what. I can see what, perhaps, clearly enough. But who are you? It's no use saying you know who you are just because you tell me you can fit your particular key into a partic- ular slot which will only receive your particular key because that's not fool- proof and certainly not conclusive. Just because you're inclined to make these statements of faith has nothing to do with me. It's not my business. Occasion- ally I believe I perceive a little of what you are but that's pure accident. Pure accident on both our parts, the perceived and the perceiver. It's nothing like an accident, it's deliberate, it's a joint pretense. We depend on these acci- dents, on these contrived accidents, to continue. It's not important then that it's conspiracy, or hallucination. What you are, or appear to be to me, or appear to be to you, changes so quickly, so horrifyingly, I certainly can't keep up with it, and I'm damn sure you can't either. But who you are I can't even begin to recognize, and sometimes I recognize it so wholly, so forcibly, I can't look, and how can I be certain of what I see? You have no number. Where am I to look, where am I to look, what is there to locate, so as to have some surety, to have some rest from this whole bloody racket? You're the scum of so many reflections. How many reflections? Whose reflections? Is that what you consist of? What scum does the tide leave? What happens to the scum? When does it happen? I've seen what happens. But I can't speak when I see it. I can only point a finger. I can't even do that. The scum is broken and sucked back. I don't see where it goes. I don't see when, what do I see, what have I seen? What have I seen, the scum or the essence? What about it?[53]

Mark is unmoved by the questions about personality until his vanity is pricked when Len, accidentally or deliberately, lets slip that Pete thinks Mark is a fool. After this incident Len is in a hospital, visited by Mark and Pete, who are clearly at odds with each other while, at the same time, realizing that in some curious way they need each other. When Len comes out of the hospital, the dwarfs are preparing to leave him, and at the end of the play they have left. So also, apparently, have Pete and Mark. The yard is clean and bare—except for a redeeming flower:

Now all is bare. All is clean. All is scrubbed. There is a lawn. There is a shrub. There is a flower.[54]

XV   *Critical Reaction to* The Dwarfs

The difficulties of staging a radio play are always interesting, but the critical response to this play, in print, and possibly heard previously, was disappointing. It was staged with *The Lover,* also in print and previously seen on television. The easier play to watch and write about was, obviously, *The Lover,* and it was that play that predominated in reviews; but, with the exception of *The New Statesman,* which simply gave a garbled version of the plot in two lines, most reviewers tackled *The Dwarfs* fairly, as far as the number of lines given to it.

David Nathan, in the *Daily Herald* (September 19), decided that he "had not got the password to Mr. Pinter's private though poetic world. Shortly afterwards I lost even the wish to enter it, and dreamed my own dreams while waiting passively for the curtain to fall." In varying degrees of agreement with Nathan were the critics of the *Daily Telegraph,* the *Guardian,* the *Spectator, Punch,* and even Harold Hobson in *The Sunday Times.* The critic of *The Times* (September 20) connected both plays with an "incurable obsession with the elusiveness of reality" and out-Pintered Pinter with a final comment: "The resolution of the play comes when Len discovers a flower in his backyard: an undeniable object."

T. C. Worsley, in the *Financial Times,* seems to have been right when he suggested that the play demanded more of an audience, including critics, than the average one was prepared to give. But he suggested that there was a reward in listening to the "heightened prose of a quite remarkable quality." He also pointed out that the play was not quite adjusted to the stage, a point raised by Bamber Gascoigne, in the *Observer,* who found the images muffled and blurred. Taylor, however, in *Plays and Players* (November 1963), felt that the transfer from radio to stage had come off better than one could have hoped for because of the density of the writing and the switches from subjective to objective moods. For a critic, Taylor offered an unusual conclusion: "The result is that one does not finally care about whether the play is or is not in theory "theatrical"; it is a riveting experience in the theater, and that, after all, is what really counts."

But the play was not new, and, even if it had been it is the job of a critic to express an opinion that will guide those people who have to pay for their tickets. We have a right to expect, even in a daily newspaper, more than a brief glance at the plot or a tentative foray into symbolic logic. Most of the reviewers who recognized that the play was "poetic" failed to give the language the attention such a recognition predicates. It is fascinating, for example, to connect the "bullock" image in *A Slight Ache* with the "bullock" image in *The Lover*. The language of *The Dwarfs* is less vernacular than we expect from Pinter; and of all his plays hints at a foreign origin. Kitchin remarked on the coincidence between *The Dwarfs* and the crabs in Sartre's *Altona* (1959): " . . . There is the feeling that this is tapping a big continental thing, and not just a parochial, though you bring it . . . you make it English that for me is a pleasure . . . you absolutely digest it."[55] This Englishness is crucial. But the work that springs to mind is, of course, Sartre's *Nausea,* and we might do well to take Iris Murdoch's advice on the interpretation of that novel:

The rich overabundance of reality, the phantasmagoria of "disordered" sensation, seem to the author of *La Nausée* a horrifying rather than a releasing spectacle, a threat to the possibility of meaning and truth. The more surprising contents of our consciousness are to be interpreted as distorted versions of our deep intentions and *not as dependent symbols* [italics mine], and certainly not as strays from a subterranean region of supreme power and value. Sartre fears, not loves, this notion of a volcanic otherness within the personality.[56]

Transferring the play from radio to the stage solved certain problems: the stage production makes clear which speeches are soliloquy and which are monologues with Pete or Mark present. Pinter's production also cleared up Taylor's difficulty over the end of the play. Taylor, comparing Len with Aston in *The Caretaker,* suggested that Len still has Aston's desperate remedy to come, hovering as he is on the brink of mental insanity: " . . . When we leave him [he] is perhaps already in a mental home. (Or is he? It depends whether Pete is being evasive when he says that Len is in hospital suffering from 'kidney' trouble, or simply stating a fact.)"[57] Pinter's production showed the last speech spoken by a Len discharged from the hospital and back home (cured?)—a fact that may color our interpretation of the last speech; which certainly, to me, gave the end an upward shift—a sense of peace, beauty, and hopefulness.

XVI   *The Meaning of* The Dwarfs

Was this sense of uplift appropriate? The meaning of *The Dwarfs* depends on how you answer two questions: is the end a victory or a defeat for Len, and who or what are the dwarfs? Both questions are essentially the same, and an optimistic answer may be simply Bad Faith.

Trussler sees Pete's speech as more important than Len's because Pete knows when a dream is a dream whereas Len is losing his power of discrimination, failing to keep his distance. But if we trace philosophers from Edward through Len to Teddy in *The Homecoming* keeping ones distance is no good thing. Lenny is a cheerful and pragmatic philosopher; Teddy becomes a stranger. And by the end Len has become a stranger—at least to his friends and the dwarfs. For Gabbard, on a Freudian interpretation, Len is "a new man . . . born into an unlittered life. The new life promises to be empty of dark old houses without the light bulbs. The new life is bright. It promises to be empty of leaky old houses filled with junk. The new life is renovated."[58] But Stanley was promised a new life at the end of *The Birthday Party*. For Burkman, Len is reborn, emerging from his ordeal into a new kingdom; for Baker/Tabachnik, Len has scored a victory by ridding himself of intruders, the dwarfs who are "compounded of the threats and hatred of the 'friends'";[59] for R. F. Storch the dwarfs are "naked childhood obsessions"—the foundations of bourgeois virtues—cleanliness, order, four walls you can call your own: "Many of the tensions in an Ibsen family are due to the frightful cost of taming the dwarfs, or to the reckless refusal to tame them."[60]

Whether we accept that this play (according to Baker/Tabachnik) teems with Jewish nuances it is clearly more autobiographical than any previous play. Martin Esslin, who has read the novel version, sees the ending as a young man emerging "from the wild whirlpool of steaming adolescence into the bare, ordered world of respectability"[61] and suggests that the girl, Virginia (who anticipates Sally in *Night School* because she is a school teacher *and* a frequenter of night clubs), was excluded because she would provide a chance motivation for what must be seen as an inevitable change, part of growing up. The dwarfs, then, represent not unseen powers or poetic imagination but simply the misery of change, the end of a relationship which leaves Len— unable to move with the times—in an antiseptic world of dead emotions.

Mark and Pete may, of course, be projections of conflicting selves in Len. Yet they are also typical Pinter characters—inconsequential in conversation, avoiding real communication or real questions as much as possible. They shun the truth, ignoring Len's unusual behavior until Mark's vanity is pricked. Each thinks, or says, that the other is bad for Len and both gull and spider are, in their different ways, predators, scavengers, feeding on corpses. Len, as the central character, may possibly be the only character. He seems to be nearly mad, anticipating what, we assume, Aston was like before his operation and echoing previous examiners—like Edward in *A Slight Ache*. The question remains, who are you?

Len cannot bear relativity: his love of mathematics, his almost Freudian concern with his bowel movements, his worry about flux in nature bring him to some kind of breakdown. We ordinarily presume that beneath the spurious permanency naming confers upon objects, there is a more absolute kind of permanency, what Miss Murdoch calls "a subterranean region of supreme power and value"—but is there? It is not so much that Len has lost poetry or sanity but that by standing still he has refused the new roles—to grow up and on. Sex would have made the recognition of this too obviously; it would have distracted the audience from a natural change which is being observed, regretfully, but implacably. Pinter is dealing with characters trying to make the crucial adjustment to society and the people they meet. If they can adjust there will be time for them to play adult games (like sex or even politics), as we shall see in *The Collection* or *The Lover*. But so far the characters have not succeeded; as is illustrated in Pinter's first really successful long play, *The Caretaker*, which is still about a room and three people.

CHAPTER 4

The Caretaker

THE connections between *The Dwarfs* and *The Caretaker* are obviously more than chronology (both appeared in 1960); the novel probably contained the seeds of both. In *The Dwarfs* Len is looking after a place for Mark and Pete tries to wean him away from a dangerous friendship, as Mick separates Aston from Davies. The links run through much of Pinter's work. As Bamber Gascoigne pointed out, in the *Observer*, "Like Stanley in *The Birthday Party*, Len is paranoic; like Aston in *The Caretaker* he ends up being straightened out in hospital, until his vision is neat, sterilised, normal." But there is another source, too. In the winter of 1958 Pinter wrote *The Hothouse*, though it was neither performed nor published. Esslin suggests that it was intended as a play for radio and indeed the large cast and five sets, unusual for a stage play by Pinter, seem to confirm this. At any rate Pinter discarded it for reasons given in an interview much later:

> It was heavily satirical and it was quite useless. I never began to like any of the characters, they didn't really live at all. So I discarded the play at once. The characters were purely cardboard. I was intentionally—for the only time I think—trying to make a point, an explicit point, that these were nasty people and I disapproved of them. And therefore they didn't begin to live. Whereas in other plays of mine every single character, even a bastard like Goldberg in *The Birthday Party*, I care for.[1]

But as he explains in an interview with John Barber in the *Daily Telegraph* (June 23, 1980), when, in 1979, he came across the script and read it as a stranger he wondered why it had not been done. Nothing about it seemed twenty years old; indeed, Pinter felt that it was more pertinent now than in 1958, when we knew nothing about Russian psychiatric hospitals. So he decided to direct it himself at the Hampstead Theatre, in May 1980 and publish the text simultaneously, "with a few cuts but no changes."

The Hothouse is a play in two acts set in a government "rest home" on Christmas Day. The inmates have no names, only numbers, while the staff, inefficiently led by an ex-army officer called Roote, rejoices in monosyllabic names like Lush, Tubb, and Lobb. It is, even for a mental home, an odd establishment. As the play opens Gibbs is telling Roote that 6457 is dead. It is fairly obvious that the efficient Gibbs intends to replace Roote as head of the establishment just as, possibly, Roote replaced *his* predecessor (the pause before "retired" in the line "When my predecessor . . . retired" encourages speculation). The newest member of the staff, Lamb, has been there nearly a year without knowing why or how he got there or who he has replaced, but he has just made a breakthrough (as he thinks) because Miss Cutts has asked him to play table tennis with her. Meanwhile Gibbs has delivered another blow to Roote's idea of an orderly establishment by announcing that 6459 has given birth to a son (it is, after all, Christmas). Roote, dumbstruck, insists that Gibbs must discover the father, though this will not be easy since 6459 has had relations with most of the staff in the last year. Naturally Gibbs chooses the most unlikely candidate, Lamb, and isolates him by inviting him to take part in an experiment. Apparently Lamb's predecessor also assisted Gibbs and Miss Cutts, which possibly explains why he left. Lamb, very eager to please, is put in a soundproof room with electrodes and earphones and is interrrogated by Miss Cutts. The act ends leaving Lamb sitting quite still as a red light in the room flashes on and off. The material for this interrogation was used by Pinter in the revue sketch "Applicant." It might be significant that Lamb's job in the establishment is to check all the locks, internal and external, at regular intervals.

In Act Two various Christmas celebrations are taking place. Roote is getting drunk with Lush (who in his own way may also be after Roote's job) when Gibbs announces that the father of the child is Lamb (who has also won the duck in the canteen raffle, though of course he is in no position to claim it). A scene follows in which Miss Cutts plays ping-pong with Gibbs, whom she wants to murder her lover, Roote, and replace him. But Gibbs seems unwilling and is disturbed, moreover, by the feeling that something is happening outside his efficient control, hinted at by frequent strange, amplified sighs and groans throughout the play—though again these may simply be the sound of the overefficient central heating which keeps this floor of the establishment literally a hothouse. Violence continues to break out—Lush and Gibbs both carry knives—and gifts (a Christmas cake and an exploding cigar) are given to Roote, who is visited by Miss Cutts, now wearing a nightdress given to her by 6459. The act reaches it climax with the delivery to staff, understaff, and inmates of Roote's Christmas message. After the blackout that follows this we see Gibbs reporting to the Ministry. It appears that the staff have all been stabbed or strangled, presumably by the patients, whose locks have not been checked. According to Gibbs, Roote was unpopular because he had seduced 6459 and murdered 6457. Gibbs is now in charge of the home, and the play ends with the tableau of Lamb still sitting quietly in the soundproof room, "as in a catatonic trance."

James Fenton, in *The Sunday Times* 4, May 1980), asked two questions: why did the author reject the play in the first place and why resurrect it now? He concludes that Pinter rejected it because he already knew he could do better, but its resurrection was welcome because it was "a work full of comic invention, which clearly occupies an important transitional role in the development of the writer." Robert Cushman, in the *Observer* (May 4, 1980), felt that the play ended up making the not particularly interesting statement that there is state-subsidized terror, and anyway Pinter seemed only to be interested in the mechanics of the play. This confirmed Cushman's belief that *The Caretaker* was a glorious sidetrack whose success Pinter has never been able to repeat, remaining, therefore, a major talent writing minor plays.

The Hothouse is clearly a black comedy, and the designer has created for it a composite set, mainly in black and white, from which almost all other color has been drained (witness the familiar Van Gogh *Sunflowers* over the fireplace, bleached here to creams and browns). The audience laughed quite a lot. Pinter described it as an odd mixture of "laughter and chill," to which we must add the ambitious sexuality in Miss Cutts, played by Angela Pleasence. This mixture returns after *The Caretaker* in the plays for television, where it is handled with more assurance than here. Pinter says that he put the play aside and then went on to write *The Caretaker*, a step that was both sensible and necessary, if we compare *The Hothouse* with, say, *The Lover* or *The Homecoming*. In rereading his play Pinter found himself laughing a lot, but as we shall see, when a critic complained that audiences were laughing at *The Caretaker* as if it were a Whitehall farce Pinter replied that the play was funny up to a point, but beyond that point it ceased to be funny, which was why he had had to write it. *The Hothouse* does not go beyond that point in any useful way.

Martin Esslin describes it as a play in which Aston's experience in the hospital has "been wildly heightened and exaggerated to form the subject matter of an entire play."[2] He also claims that the play contained the name "Jenkins" but this seems not to have survived in the published version. Certainly the bearing on *The Caretaker* is as clear, if less obvious, than the reuse of material in "Applicant." Esslin explains Pinter's early rejection as being part of the recognition that the future lay in realism, not fantasy—an opposite view to that of Robert Cushman, who regards *The Caretaker* as an isolated deviation. Certainly it must have been the relatively straightforward nature of *The Caretaker* that helped to account for its success. Howard Taubman, in the *New York Times* (October 1961), described it as a play of "strangely compelling beauty and passion" and its author as "one of the important playwrights of our day." Clifford Leech saw it as "the most impressive dramatic writing in England since the war,"[3] while Laurence Kitchen admired the way foreign influences had been thrown off and wider allusions "to the affluent society's materialism and cruelty to its casualties" occurred.[4] The first French production was not successful, however ("Either [the play] is an imposture, or the British have gone mad"), but a new production in 1969 suggested that the first production had not helped the play and confirmed the greatness of *Le Gardien*. So while *The Dwarfs* remained enigmatic *The Caretaker*, in spite of its brief initial run, marked the beginning of Pinter's public recognition—which, moreover, encouraged another look at the earlier plays.

As far as Pinter himself is concerned, the play is simply the extension of his basic idea, encouraged, presumably, by his experience tending a boiler in Notting Hill Gate: "I went into a room and saw one person standing up and one person sitting down, and a few weeks later I wrote *The Room*. I went into another room and saw two people sitting down, and a few years later [?] I wrote *The Birthday Party*. I looked through a door into a third room, and saw two people standing up and I wrote *The Caretaker*."[5] If it is a simple play it is also difficult to talk about it without making some reference to hypotheses about the action. Rattigan's allegorical view may be far-fetched, but Esslin sees Mick as the snake who gets Adam expelled from Paradise and throws in father-figures and Oedipal desires for good measure.[6] Gabbard extends these last with Freudian inevitability so that even the plug Aston is fiddling with becomes a phallus substitute![7] Aston has Christological associations—his age, his profession, and his suffering—and the whole play takes place in a room full of junk which might *mean* something; the bucket does, and the Buddha should. On the other hand it may fulfill Artaud's dictum that the stage is a space to be filled, and our desire to make it mean something reflects our view that things in life cannot simply exist, they must signify. If the setting and the events of the play are closely related to the actual world, both the speech and behavior operate in the world of fantasy. And Pinter has observed that "the one thing that people have missed is that it isn't necessary to conclude that everything Aston says about his experience in the mental hospital is true."[8]

Noticeably, too, violence has been largely eliminated in a physical sense—there are only practical jokes played on Davies by Mick (who is well named since he does "take the Mick" out of poor Davies). Originally the play was to have ended with the violent death of the tramp:

It suddenly struck me that it was not necessary. And I think that in this play I have developed, that I have no need to use cabaret turns and blackouts and screams in the dark to the extent that I enjoyed using them before. I feel that I can deal, without resorting to that kind of thing, with a human situation. I do see this play as merely a particular human situation, concerning three particular people, and not, incidentally, symbols.[9]

Pinter told Charles Marowitz that the subject was love; it may be that Pleasance's summary is just as revealing: boy meets tramp, boy loses tramp.

I *The Action of the Play*

A young man in his twenties, named Mick, wearing a leather jacket, is surveying the room. We must associate a black leather jacket (in 1960) with fascism, or Marlon Brando in *The Wild One*. When he hears voices approaching the room he leaves, and Aston, a man in his early thirties, enters, accompanied by a tramp who calls himself MacDavies and whom Aston has just rescued from a fight in a café. Aston, a slow-witted but kindly man, offers Davies a bed for the night. Davies very quickly emerges from his conversation as an opinionated, bigoted, irascible old layabout whose perpetual chatter contrasts sharply with Aston's taciturnity and is often fostered by it.

Davies's conversation, whether we believe it or not, tells us of his employment in a café where he was "put on" by the colored customers;

of his hatred of dirt (he left his wife a fortnight after the marriage ostensibly because he found her underwear in the vegetable pan); of his hatred of Blacks, Greeks, and Poles—and particularly Blacks; of his feeling that the world owes him a living and particularly a pair of shoes (if we do not believe the story of the monastery at Luton we do recognize the need for good shoes and his habit, even in his circumstances, of being choosy). Thus the shoes that Aston offers him in the play are usually the wrong color, shape, or material; or they have no shoelaces—details that in Davies's present state seem ludicrously insisted upon. Davies is not merely homeless, he has even lost his identity. In answer to the question, "Who are you?" he would have to reply that he is called Jenkins at present, but if he could get down to Sidcup where his papers are. . . . Aston, we learn, likes to work with his hands, wants to clear the garden and build a shed, can only drink Guinness from a thin glass, and collects junk almost compulsively, the centerpiece of which is a Buddha, chosen, again, because it is well made.

From the first night it is obvious that these two men will not be able to live in harmony. The tramp Davies keeps Aston awake at night with his jabbering and dreams, both of which he angrily denies in the morning and attributes to the blacks next door. On the other hand Davies is uneasy in this room full of junk, bewildered by Aston's references to machines—to a jig-saw, to plugging in the electric fire, or learning to use the vacuum cleaner. He is even apprehensive of the gas stove, although it is not connected to the mains. Aston's conversation, too, is not helpful or easy to follow. He can move from the discussion of some new tool he wants to pick up to the story of a woman in a café who wanted to have a look at his body. Davies finds it difficult to find the suitable reply. He talks, however, of finding a job (or going down to Sidcup) but is quite content to do nothing. As soon as Aston leaves he starts poking about the flat, trying to find some meaning (or financial value?) in the accumulated junk. As he is doing this, Mick reenters and throws him to the floor with the brisk question, "What's the game?"

In Act Two, a few seconds later, the trouserless Davies is still on the floor, but Mick is transformed into a smooth, polite, very friendly Cockney who is glad to hear that Davies slept well and who is awfully glad to meet him. Mick's conversation, rapid and fluent, is as terrifying to Davies as Aston's silence. Mick insists on comparing Davies with someone else, though who is not clear in the positive barrage of information:

You know, believe it or not, you've got a funny kind of resemblance to a bloke I once knew in Shoreditch. Actually he lived in Aldgate. I was staying with a cousin in Camden Town. This chap, he used to have a pitch in Finsbury Park, just by the bus depot. When I got to know him I found out he was brought up in Putney. That didn't make any difference to me. I know quite a few people who were born in Putney. Even if they weren't born in Putney they were born in Fulham. The only trouble was, he wasn't born in Putney, he was only brought up in Putney. It turned out he was born in the Caledonian Road, just before you get to the Nag's Head. His old mum was still living at the Angel. All the buses passed right by the door. She could get a 38, 581, 30 or 38A, take her down the Essex Road to Dalston Junction in next to no time. Well, of course, if she got the 30 he'd take her up Upper Street way, round Highbury Corner and down to St. Paul's Church, but she'd get to Dalston Junction just the same in the end. I used to leave my bike in her garden on my way to work. Yes, it was a curious affair. Dead spit of you he was. Bit bigger round the nose but there was nothing in it.[10]

All of which tells poor Davies nothing. What is worse, not only does Mick insist on confusing him with other people, but he also tells Davies that the house is his, and the room, and even the bed Davies slept in, which he offers to sell for a fair price. This bargain is interrupted only by the return of Aston with a bag of things for Davies. After a piece of byplay with the bag between the two brothers and the unfortunate Davies (strongly reminiscent of the scene with Lucky's hat in *Waiting for Godot*), Mick leaves, and Aston, explaining nothing exept that Mick is his brother and has a sense of humor, offers Davies the job of caretaker when the room has been decorated. Davies, reasonably enough in the circumstances, is evasive, particularly about answering enquiries at the door and about having his name on a card:

Of course I got plenty of other cards lying about, but they don't know that and I can't tell them, can I, because then they'd find out I was going about under an assumed name. You see, the name I call myself now, that's not my real name. My real name's not the one I'm using, you see. It's different. You see, the name I go under now ain't my real one. It's assumed.[11]

The next scene begins with the entry of Davies into a darkened room where the lights will not work and where a figure begins to hunt him with a vacuum cleaner. Suddenly the light goes on, and Mick plausibly explains that he has been doing a bit of spring cleaning. He offers the frightened, rather hostile Davies a sandwich and begins to confide in him by asking his advice, for Davies, as he says, is a man of the world. First Mick introduces the subject of his brother, who is funny (although Mick, ominously, turns sharply on Davies when the latter agrees that he is); second, the decorating of the house, which will need a caretaker. Assured that Davies has references at Sidcup, Mick offers him the job and leaves; and, in the next scene, Davies, beginning to feel confident and powerful from these discoveries (and quite overlooking Mick's changeable moods), begins to quibble with Aston about his bed and the window.

Aston, however, is not really listening. Half to Davies and half to himself, he speaks of the time in his life when he used to see things clearly, talk to people, and mix with them, until one day he was sent to a hospital for examination. There the doctor told him that he was ill and that something would have to be done to his mind so that he could go out and "live like the others." When his mother gave permission for this treatment he tried to escape; and, when he was caught, he tried to prevent the shock treatment by standing upright—but they administered the shock anyway, and he went home. But his thoughts had become slow and uncertain, and he could neither move his head nor write:

And I laid everything out, in order, in my room, all the things I knew were mine, but I didn't die. I never had those hallucinations any more. And I never spoke to anyone any more. The funny thing is, I can't remember much . . . about what I said, what I thought . . . I mean before I went into that place. The thing is I should have been dead. I should have died. And then, anyway, after a time, I got a bit better, and I started to do things with my hands, and then about two years ago I came here, because my brother had got this house and so I decided to have a go at decorating it, so I came into this room, and I started to collect wood, for my shed, and all these bits and pieces, that I thought might come in handy for the flat, or around the house, sometime. I feel much better now. But I don't talk to people now. I don't talk to anyone . . . like that. I've often thought of going back and trying to find the man who did that to me. But I want to do something first. I want to build that shed out in the garden.[12]

The sad truth is that Aston *has* talked, as he used to, confidingly.

Two weeks later, Davies, confident of his position in the room, talks quite openly to Mick about Aston's failings and encourages Mick to reveal his plans for turning the room into a luxury flat, a penthouse in the very latest style:

I'd have teal-blue, copper and parchment linoleum squares. I'd have those colors re-echoed in the walls. I'd offset the kitchen units with charcoal-grey worktops. Plenty of room for cupboards for the crockery. We'd have a small wall cupboard, a large wall cupboard, a corner wall cupboard with revolving shelves. You wouldn't be short of cupboards. You could put the dining-room across the landing, see? Yes. Venetian blinds, venetian blinds on the window, cork floor, cork tiles. You could have an off-white pile linen rug, a table in . . . in afromosia teak veneer, sideboard with matt black drawers, curved chairs with cushioned seats, armchairs in oatmeal tweed, beech frame settee with woven sea-grass seat, white-topped heat-resistant coffee table, white tile surround. Yes. Then the bedroom. What's a bedroom? It's a retreat. It's a place to go for rest and peace. So you want quiet decoration. The lighting functional. Furniture . . . mahogany and rosewood. Deep azure-blue carpet, unglazed blue and white curtains, a bedspread with a pattern of small blue roses on a white ground, dressing table with a lift-up top containing a plastic tray, table lamp of white raffia . . . (MICK *sits up*) it wouldn't be a flat it'd be a palace.[13]

But Davies is not really listening to Mick's dream. He presses on with his own demands—a clock to tell the time by, for example—principally, that Mick should speak to his brother, who is disturbing Davies at night and annoying him. But when Aston enters, Mick leaves as usual. The shoes that Aston produces are unsatisfactory, and Aston wakes Davies that night because he is making noises. Davies, annoyed at being awakened in the middle of the night, taunts Aston with the memory of the hospital:

They can put them pincers on your head again, man! They can have them on again! Any time. All they got to do is get the word. They'd carry you in there, boy. They'd come here and pick you up and carry you in! They'd keep you fixed! They'd put them pincers on your head, they'd have you fixed! They'd take one look at all this junk I got to sleep with they'd know you were a creamer. That was the greatest mistake they made, you take my tip, letting you get out of that place. . . .[14]

When Aston quietly tells Davies that he had better go, Davies plays his trump card—Mick's offer of a job as caretaker. It will be Aston who goes. But Aston firmly puts him out, defeating attempts by Davies at violence.

The next scene shows Davies and Mick in the room. Mick is smooth and polite, but he points out immediately that Davies does get a bit out of his depth. Davies now finds that he is expected to be an interior decorator: which he denies, insisting that Mick must have the wrong man. But Mick replies, "How could I have the wrong man? You're the only man I've spoken to. You're the only man I've told, about my dreams, about my deepest wishes, you're the only one I've told, and I only told you because I understood you were an experienced first-class professional interior and exterior decorator."[15]

And when Davies calls Aston "nutty" Mick turns on him and dismisses him:

What a strange man you are. Aren't you? You're really strange. Ever since you come into this house there's been nothing but trouble. Honest. I can take nothing you say at face value. Every word you speak is open to any number of different interpretations. Most of what you say is lies. You're violent, you're erratic, you're just completely unpredictable. You're nothing else but a wild animal, when you come down to it. You're a barbarian. And to put the old tin lid on it, you stink from arse-hole to breakfast time. Look at it. You come here recommending yourself as an interior decorator, whereupon I take you on, and what happens? You make a long speech about all the references you've got down at Sidcup, and what happens? I haven't noticed you go down to Sidcup to obtain them. It's all most regrettable but it looks as though I'm compelled to pay you off for your caretaking work. Here's half a dollar.[16]

Then, in a fit of anger, Mick washes his hands of house, Davies, and brother by smashing the Buddha. Aston enters, but the brothers do not speak; they smile faintly at each other, and Mick leaves.[17] Davies now tries to reconcile himself with Aston but Aston is unmoved, and the play ends with Davies's pathetic reference to the papers at Sidcup, which, presumably, fails.

II   *What the Play Is About*

The play is about, apparently, two brothers and Davies, and how we interpret their relationship depends upon the tone, upon performance. For Pinter even bus routes are beautiful and elegiac. Baker/Tabachnik point out how Davies's dialogue has the power "to excite at once the audience's sadistic tendencies and its pity": "He is a man bargaining with Fate with absolutely no leverage except his rattled brains and finally his knife on his side, a Charlie Chaplin ne'er-do-well who lacks the saving grace of a good heart."[18] When Mick smashes the Buddha he momentarily sides with Davies, who understands brutality more than charity; but his speech about having to look after his brother betrays his acceptance that he is his brother's keeper whether he likes it or not; and the look that passes between Aston and Mick seals Davies's fate. It is, as some critics have remarked, not enthusiastic, but only "faint"—but then the same could be said of the smile of the Mona Lisa. It hints at complicity. And Aston's single long speech, where the dividing line between truth and fantasy is thin gives definition to that relationship. As Trussler comments, it explains "the dramatic necessity for Mick's intermittent appearances, *taking care* of Aston, which would otherwise by merely functional—and it motivates Davies's intended shift in allegiance. Far from not having listened to Aston's story, as he tells Mick, Davies was, in fact, taking in every word,"[19] and he soon throws them back in Aston's face in the longest speech he has. But then for Davies, liar that he is, the recognition that truth and fantasy are not divided is easy. He is rejected because he rejects. It is difficult to forgive him but the play ends on a question, which is not really whether Davies will get to Sidcup or Aston build his shed, but whether the audience can answer Davies's last plea which hangs in the air, still, as the curtain falls.

The problem in performance was to reconcile this serious and moving story with the rich vein of comedy. Leonard Russell in *The Sunday Times* was disturbed by an audience that laughed as if it were a Whitehall farce. Pinter answered this in a letter published on August 14, 1960:

Certainly I laughed myself while writing "The Caretaker" but not all the time, not "indiscriminately." An element of the absurd it is, I think, one of the features of the play, but at the same time I did not intend it to be merely a laughable farce. If there hadn't been other issues at stake the play would not have been written.

Audience reaction can't be regulated, and no one would want it to be; nor is it easy to analyse. But where the comic and the tragic (for want of a better word) are closely interwoven, certain members of an audience will always give emphasis to the comic as opposed to the other, for by so doing they rationalize the other out of existence.

Pinter saw this indiscriminate laughter as a kind of smoke screen the audience throws up to protect itself and he dissociates himself from it:

As far as I am concerned, "The Caretaker" is funny, up to a point. Beyond that point it ceases to be funny, and it was because of that point that I wrote it.

The laughter is obviously qualified. The surprising thing is that in spite of his character and behavior it is possible to feel sympathy for Davies at the end of the play. The organizing factor is the dialogue, which moves easily from completely naturalistic talk into fantasy, working by a contrast of verbosity and taciturnity, both evasions in the matter of communication. On all sides, the questions being asked are who has power over me and who am I? There is no sex to confuse the issue, except for Aston's briefly related encounter with a woman in a café (which may or may not be true), no social life (although Mick must go somewhere in his van and Aston did pick up Davies in a café), and no politics (though Davies's extreme racist views do introduce a very modern note to the play): there are no ideas, simply people living very much alone.

III   *The Film of* The Caretaker

The film, renamed *The Guest* in America, made with Donald Pleasance and Alan Bates from the original cast and Robert Shaw replacing Peter Woodthorpe as Aston,[20] removes some ambiguities but remains, with sensitive direction from Clive Donner, a Pinter kind of film. It was the work of a dedicated team, shot on location at Hackney for only £30,000 without any guarantee of distribution, and financed privately with a list of backers ranging from Noel Coward and Elizabeth Taylor to the continuity girl. It was shown at the Edinburgh Festival and later at the Academy Cinema in London.

Pinter and Donner discussed the film in an article published in the summer of 1963.[21] In it they raised the three points any such translation from stage to film must involve: was the play cinematic, did the film open the play out, and did that opening out lead to the inclusion of an exterior life, never denied in the play but apparently excluded by the claustrophobic atmosphere and themes? Pinter suggested that the conflicts of the play provided a situation that must be "exciting cinema." And he welcomed the opening out because it allowed him to do things that, without knowing it, he had yearned to do when writing for the stage:

For instance, there's a scene in the garden of the house, which is very silent; two silent figures with a third looking on. I think in the film one has been able to hit the relationship of the brothers more clearly than in the play.

He was also pleased at being able, in the film, to put the play into the context of the outside world:

... We see a real house and real snow outside, dirty snow and the streets. We don't see them very often but they're there, the backs of houses and windows, attics in the distance. There is actually sky as well, a dirty one, and these characters move in the context of a real world—as I believe they do. In the play, when people were confronted with just a set, a room and a door, they often assumed it was all taking place in limbo, in a vacuum, and the world outside hardly existed, or had existed at some point but was only half remembered.

Pinter was asked, elsewhere, whether or not this translation from the stage to the essentially visual, naturalistic medium of the cinema had not altered the play and he thought not. The limitations of the stage imposed the set upon him but he had also taken it for granted that there was a world outside and was perturbed that some people had assumed there was not and changed the characters into allegorical fictions—"the devil and . . . materialism and . . . mankind and God and Christ"—whereas the location of the play was "a room in a house in a street in a town in the world."[22] Thus, as Pinter points out, we actually see Mick's van, a real van in a real street. The film, therefore, removed at least one ambiguity, although it was an ambiguity that Pinter would prefer to be without and had never intended. The assumption by audiences that the play takes place in a kind of vacuum had been a kind of triumph for Pinter of theme over the stage illusion of the set; in most plays we assume that there are rooms offstage. The interpolations in the film—street scenes, a visit to a secondhand clothes shop, the garden scenes with a coffin-shaped fish pond, even breakfast in a café with Mick—do not alter the play; they remind us of what we should never have forgotten in the first place. And there is one superb addition to replace the curtain that falls after Aston's long and harrowing speech. This new scene breaks the tension without destroying the emotion. Davies, sitting on a roadside bench, is picked up by the ebullient Mick in his van and threatened with a visit to Sidcup. The horror this suggestion produces is immediately dissipated in laughter as Mick solemnly drives Davies around a traffic island, depositing him where he found him with excuses about heavy traffic and a shortage of gas!

The greatest danger of filming a play which relies as drama very much on the dialogue is that whereas in a theater people do listen fairly attentively, in the cinema many effects are achieved too glibly and by visual means. The adaptation is acute in recognizing what the cinema does and does not require. As Taylor points out, the additions, largely of wordless exteriors, "have the proper effect of emphasizing the intensity and isolation of the scenes in the room, rather than breaking the concentration."[23]

The earliest critical notice was by Mordecai Richler, in *Town* (December 1963), who found it a curiously bothersome film which left him with the feeling of being tricked:

> I thought the obscurity was not inherent in what Pinter has to say but essential to conceal the absence of core to *The Caretaker*. In short, shot upon significant shot of the Buddha statue, I still felt I was being artily had. However, I should add I'm in a minority.

That he *was* in a minority became clear when the film was shown in London. Penelope Gilliatt, in the *Observer* (March 15, 1964), observed that the tramp "is haunted by suspicions of malevolence, but he has no one to ask about them; so when he is talked to he often says 'What?,' not because he hasn't heard, but as a hopeless way of gaining time and puzzling out how much ground he has lost." She wondered how dramatists had managed to do without this style of dialogue for so long and praised the whole film unreservedly. Dilys Powell, in *The Sunday Times* (March 15, 1964), was equally impressed. If the film had a simple plot it was really about three solitaries in a claustrophobic room. Her comment that the tramp also has his fantasy was very pertinent; and, as she remarked, though funny the film is about very serious matters—solitude, ingratitude, and cruelty.

John Coleman, in the *New Statesman* (March 13, 1964), also praised the film as a remarkable job, very well done on a low budget. He saw Mick's motive in getting rid of the tramp not so much as resulting from annoyance at being deceived as from a desire to protect his brother— a very plausible interpretation of the film version. Coleman suggested that the film was more satisfying than the play because it touched the audience on the raw, in its fury, as he put it, "with the whole devious business of clambering over the minds of one's fellow men in search of some local self-aggrandisement." Isabel Quigly, in the *Spectator* (March 20, 1964), was similarly impressed, but she felt that the brothers threw the old man out simply because they were tired of his "nasty and obtrusive presence," an interpretation that has the virtue of simplicity as well as backing from Pleasance's portrayal.

Critics, on the whole, were impressed with the author, actors, director, and the work of the cameraman, Nicolas Roeg. The content of their criticism, moreover, showed more competency, elegance, and expertise than most drama critics had shown so far when dealing with Pinter. As John Cutts wrote in *Films and Filming* (January 1964), one can take one's pick in *The Caretaker* of a half-dozen allegories, but too severe rationalization gets in the way of enjoying the ambiguity and contradictions that make it a film that is "funny, accurate, poignant, provocative, and, at all times, unique."

IV *The Meaning of* The Caretaker

It must be obvious that no interpretation will exactly fit; if it did there would be no point in writing the play. The craftsman in Pinter shapes what his instinct troubles him with which may be a particular private problem dealt with in a universal way or a common problem presented in a particular way. Each member of the audience will use whatever key, or golden bough, will open doors and conduct him safely to hell and back. Our response to the play depends upon our interpretation of three characters, and particularly Davies, who, if unsympathetic, is still central. But in *The Caretaker* whatever private information is offered it is offered both on the level of fantasy and also on a level where comprehensible motivation, should we desire it, is available. Thus Taylor interprets the play as follows:

Mick is trying to get through to his brother, interest him in something. Davies is the first human being who has interested Aston since Aston left the mental home, and Mick, his jealousy aroused, wants to get rid of him. Mick realizes he can only do so if Aston voluntarily rejects Davies, and so he leads Davies into believing he will hire him as caretaker when the house is redecorated. Davies falls into the trap by trying to play off one brother agianst the other, by rejecting his real friend, Aston, for Mick, even going so far as telling Mick his brother is mad. Mick now rejects Davies, who tries to become reconciled with Aston, but it is too late. Aston has now determined to build his shed, and there is no place in his life for Davies, who has to leave as the curtain falls.[24]

Such an interpretation lays too narrow an emphasis on motives, gives the play an ending which it lacks, and overlooks Mick's own insecurity.

It makes Mick too much a villain and opportunist—and Davies too little of either. Nor is it true, as Taylor suggests, that only Davies is subject in his conversation to characteristic Pinter ambiguity. We had better call it that rather than truth and lies because the distinction is no longer a clear one as Pinter suggested in a program note for the Royal Court:

The desire for verification is understandable, but cannot always be satisfied. There are no hard distinctions between what is real and what is unreal, nor between what is true and what false. The assumption that to verify what has happened and what is happening presents few problems, I take to be inaccurate. A character on the stage who can present no convincing argument or information as to his past experiences, his present behavior or his aspirations, nor give a comprehensive analysis of his motives is as legitimate and as worthy of attention as one who, alarmingly, can do all these things.

The keyword, surely, is "alarmingly." It questions the basis of the well-made play; and yet, as John Arden has pointed out, Pinter's method of writing with the corners never quite joined up is as carefully constructed as the so-called well-made play. Arden also rejected allegory:

Taken purely at its face value this play is a study of the unexpected strength of family ties against an intruder. That in itself is a subject deep enough to carry many layers of meaning without our having to superimpose any extra scheme of Symbols. . . .[25]

On the stage these two brothers do not strike us as characters from *Paradise Lost* but simply as two brothers whom we could meet on the street. Cosmic implications ought not to be smuggled in from Beckett or Ionesco. The characters here grumble, fight about who shall sleep where, and make vague plans—as in naturalistic drama. Two questions move the action of the play: Mick wants to know who this tramp is with his brother, and Davies wants to know who has the power to throw him out. Such questions involve love, politics, relationships, and domination. We do not need Freud to remind us that dreams are contexts in which we give ourselves away, not illusions. Or that illusions are necessary to protect us from a reality that humankind cannot bear too much of. Life, after all, is like a major operation; we would not want to go through it without an anaesthetic. This dual quality of fantasy operates most pertinently in the area of sexual experience—to which Pinter now turns.

CHAPTER 5

Comedy of Manners

P INTER first explored comedy of manners in plays written for television. Of course the shift from theater to television introduces two
factors, the medium and the audience. The former is remarkably flex-
ible while the latter is almost impossible to define, though its very size
invites a low estimate of its expectations. Pinter was not merely given
mobility of scene and location by television; he was also, by use of the
camera, given mobility of point of view by, for example, the use of
close-up. Nowadays the dramatist is less than ever restricted to the
theater. Indeed economic pressures frequently drive him into the more
lucrative spheres of television and the cinema, where the audience is,
potentially, even larger. Pinter's work for television seems to have
encouraged audiences to find him acceptable, and this helped to create
a climate of opinion favorable to his stage plays as well as modifying
his methods of writing.

I   *A New Kind of Play*

The size of Pinter's audiences on television probably proves nothing,
though it does suggest that his plays could be experienced on several
levels. Clearly the elegant, comfortable settings looking out on to a
sunny garden helped (though this set had been used in *A Slight Ache*)
and were more congenial than the old, sick, and shabby world of the
early plays. There the inescapable echoes of Beckett and Greene had
tended to contradict Pinter's own assertion that what happened in his
plays could happen anywhere, anytime, and in anybody's life even if
the events seemed unfamiliar at first glance.

Pinter was quick to recognize the different possibilities and demands
of writing for television:

I don't make any distinction between kinds of writing, but when I write for the stage I always keep a continuity of action. Television lends itself to quick cutting from scene to scene, and nowadays I see it more and more in terms of pictures. Of course the words go with the pictures, but on television, ultimately, the words are of less importance than they are on the stage.[1]

Pinter will perfect this technique of "quick cutting" in his film work and ultimately incorporate it into his stage plays. Nor does he find television restrictive in the expectations of an audience. Since one of his plays had an audience of 16 million people it is obviously not a showcase to be ignored.

In this chapter we shall look at the first three plays written specifically for television as opposed to plays translated into that medium. The obvious differences are in atmosphere, characters, and setting. The wit grows more elegant, the comedy more comic, and sex is the mainspring of this new world. In a sense television liberated Pinter from his room and sent him off to Sidcup. The first play written for television, however, was something of a setback. *A Night Out*, written for radio, had been quickly transferred to television and performed successfully in April 1960. Soon after, on July 21, the first play for television, *Night School*, was performed. Pinter felt it was not a successful piece of writing. However, he went on to write *The Collection* (televised in May 1961) and *The Lover* (televised in March 1963), both of which have been staged subsequently.

II   Night School

Pinter said of *Night School*: "Later I realised that in one short television play of mine there were characteristics that implied I was slipping into a formula. It so happened this was the worst thing I've written. The words and ideas had become automatic, redundant. That was the red light for me and I don't feel I shall fall into that pit again."[2] When Pinter sent me a copy I felt he was perhaps being overly severe, and he has come to think so, too, since he revised the play in the summer of 1966 and allowed it to be published in 1967. Some of the wit is unfortunate, as when Solto romances about his early experiences to the two aunts:

SOLTO: And what a trip. I was only a pubescent. I killed a man with my own hands, a six foot ten Lascar from Madagascar.
ANNIE: From Madagascar?

SOLTO: Sure. A lascar.
ANNIE: Alaska?
SOLTO: Madagascar.

But even this cliché joke is well placed in the play and not without value as cliché. Similarly, there is the familiar pun on "tart":

> I bet you never had a tart in prison,
> Wally?
> No, I couldn't lay my hands on one.

Here we have part of an extensive system of food references with sexual implications which reflect the failure of communication.

Night School is chiefly remarkable, however, for the flexibility television allows. Pinter is able to add to the major scenes little vignettes (much like his revue sketch material) in a way that looks forward to his work in films. The disappearance of these vignettes in the two subsequent television plays points up the difference of *Night School*—the large number of characters. In *The Collection* and *The Lover* Pinter returned to a limited number of characters.

The play opens with Wally's return home from prison to his aunts Annie and Milly after serving nine months for forging entries in Post Office Savings Bank books. The two aunts clearly have something to tell him but are uneasy. So, instead, they stuff him with food and talk about nothing. Finally they tell him that they have let his room to a young, quiet, homely girl called Sally Gibbs, a schoolteacher who goes to night school three times a week, bathes twice a day, wears lovely perfume, and knows Wally has been in prison but not why. Wally is hurt and defensive. Although he had not contributed to the aunts' living expenses, he had bought the bed Sally is sleeping in and had been looking forward to getting back to his own room. He points out that prison has accustomed him to privacy and that sleeping in the dining room will rob him of it. He meets Sally later when he goes to his old room to collect some things he left there. For her, too, the room is important—a haven, a place of peace and security. As he recovers some Post Office bank books from a secret place in the wardrobe, he accidentally discovers a photograph of Sally that suggests that she works as a hostess in a night club. As the scene ends Wally starts to practice forging signatures.

The second part introduces Solto, a scrap merchant and a friend of Wally, who is having tea with the aunts and boasting about his prowess in Australia, where he discovered cricket and Bradman, and his adventures in the merchant navy. Solto cannot, however, lend Wally the £200 he asked for even if Wally is prepared to go straight and give up the forgery for which he has no talent. When Wally shows him the photograph Solto thinks he has seen Sally somewhere and is asked by Wally to trace her. Thus, although there is every possibility that they could be friends and that Wally could regain his bed and room either by having an affair with Sally or even marrying her, Wally wants to find out the "truth." While Solto is searching a relationship is established. As the aunts eat in bed (for them, as for Solto, food is the equivalent of sex), they hear Wally visit Sally for a cup of coffee. He takes along a bottle of brandy but she pretends to be unused to drinking. She also claims that she is learning languages at night school and after class goes to a girl friend's flat to listen to records of Mozart and Brahms. Wally claims that he used to plan his armed robberies in this very room and that from being a very successful gunman he became a very successful prison librarian—so successful that the British Museum have offered him a job in charge of rare manuscripts. He also suggests that his aunts have Sally in mind as a prospective wife for him (the earlier discussion between Solto and the aunts was about Wally and marriage), but he claims he has been married three times already. This statement he immediately denies and makes Sally model for him. She stands up, crosses and uncrosses her legs. Finally he kisses her. The whole scene is remarkably close to the scene between Albert and the prostitute in *A Night Out*.

Part Three begins with Solto's visit to the night club where Sally works. A scene in the dressing room shows the unsophisticated side of Sally who is now called Katina. The camera switches to the aunts who are rejoicing that Wally is falling for her and then returns to the main scene between Sally and Solto. Solto boasts of his possessions, including a private beach. Telling her that he is looking for her, he shows her the photograph, revealing that Wally Street, forger and petty thief, wants information about her. Esslin suggests that Solto "inadvertently" reveals this, but the scene strikes me as more calculated: Solto reveals this to bring pressure to bear on Sally. Presumably she complies with his wishes, since in the next scene with Walter Solto denies finding her. By this time Wally does not want to know anyway and tells Solto to abandon the search. When they hear Sally coming in Wally says it is the schoolteacher, and Solto advises him to go after her because she is an educated girl. She will not open her door, however, to Walter and next morning she is gone, leaving a note for the aunts, the Misses Billet (in the sense of temporary lodging?). So Walter gets his room back—and finds another photograph of Sally as a schoolteacher with the volleyball team!

Night School was intended, I suspect, to be part of a movement toward light comedy and new realism. But no author should put old wine into new bottles; it exploits old themes too obviously—conflict for possession of a room (which stands for peace and security for both Wally and Sally) and lying (or fantasy). Wally lies to achieve his various purposes, and the contradictions tell us something about him; Solto lies, but the truth, or otherwise, of the stories never comes into question; and Sally also tells lies. A question posed by the play is what is Sally? That question has been answered by the end of the play—unless the last photograph is also false: she is both teacher and night club hostess but this generates, somehow, very little excitement. It should since the respectable girl who is also a whore becomes the central theme of many subsequent plays (and had its prototype in Virginia in the novel of *The Dwarfs*).

Nevertheless the play is a step forward in considering the dual reality of Sally/Katina. But Sally is also a girl who might have helped Wally more than the possession of his room will. The concentrated collection of "lies" reminds us that people act differently in different contexts; the end of the play leaves a sense of emotional loss—similar to that at the end of *The Caretaker*. What else can one expect but failure from so many inventions? To impress Sally, Wally invents a character, just as she invents a character to impress the aunts and Wally, just as Solto invents one to impress Sally. No true relationship could be based on all these deceoptions—or could it? The next play explores just such a collection.

III   The Collection

This was Pinter's second play written for television. The characters are not tramps or even ex-convicts but dress designers who have elegant rooms. There is still the comedy of menace (though it is very muted) but it is mainly a comedy of manners. The action concerns two couples: James and Stella (man and wife) and Harry and Bill (whose relationship is presumably homosexual). The play describes a series of encounters between man and wife, protector and protégé, man and protégé, and protector and wife. The action begins at four o'clock in the morning with a rather sinister telephone call from James to Bill received by Harry. Swift scenes follow between James and Stella and Harry and Bill that illustrate the tensions and uneasiness of both couples. After Harry has gone out, Bill receives a visit from James who telephones to make sure that Harry is out. James threatens Bill amiably on such matters as having no olives in the flat, but then suddenly accuses him of having slept with his wife, Stella, in Leeds the week before. Bill, amused, suggests that Stella is making it up, but when James makes a sudden aggressive movement he falls to the floor. Under pressure Bill admits that he kissed her and no more; under further pressure, he says that he did, in fact, go to bed with her.

The two short scenes that follow develop the domestic tensions in each couple (that between James and Stella revolving once more around the lack of olives), and James tells his wife that Bill has confessed. She neither confirms nor denies it, but is rather surprised to find that James likes Bill. James finds Bill intelligent, he has a collection of interesting Chinese vases, likes opera, and reminds him of a boy at school he had very much liked. So James goes off to see Bill again while Harry, worried by the effect James's attentions are having on Bill, goes to see Stella. She tells him that James has fabricated the story after two years of happy marriage and that he has never behaved like this before, though she is often away on business. Harry, happily reassured, admires her Persian kitten.

Meanwhile, James and Bill are getting on together very well although the olives Bill has provided are now rejected by James. As James muses over his wife's infidelity, he plays with a cheese knife, and, as Harry enters unnoticed, James suddenly challenges Bill to a duel, throwing the knife at him. Bill catches it clumsily, cutting himself in the process, and Harry intervenes. Introducing himself to James,[3] he says that he has just got the truth from Stella: she had made the story up (which is not what we heard!). Bill agrees, saying that he confessed only because it amused him to do so—and Harry, furiously, explains this "amusement" in an attack on Bill:

HARRY: Bill's a slum boy, you see, he's got a slum sense of humor. That's why I never take him along with me to parties. Because he's got a slum mind. I have nothing against slum minds *per se*, you understand, nothing at all. There's a certain kind of slum mind which is perfectly all right in a slum, but when this slum mind gets out of the slum it sometimes persists, you see, it rots everything. That's what Bill is. There's something faintly putrid about him, don't you find? Like a slug. There's nothing wrong with slum slugs in their place, but this one won't keep his place—he crawls over the walls of nice houses, leaving slime, don't you boy? He confirms stupid little stories just to amuse himself, while everyone else has to run round in circles to get to the root of the matter and smooth the whole thing out. All he can do is sit and suck his bloody hand and decompose like the filthy putrid slum slug he is.[4]

Clearly this humiliation of Bill by Harry tells us more about Harry than about Bill. Harry's anger and fear are those of an older man who recognizes the dangerous temptations of Stella *and* James for his younger friend. But the venom of the speech stings Bill so much that— as James and Harry are smoothing out the situation, each with a truth that satisfies, covering up the trouble with the conventional excuse of overwork; and solving it with the conventional suggestion of a holiday abroad—he suddenly insists that he will tell the Truth. He and Stella had just sat together downstairs and talked about what they would do if they went up to her room. And James has to return to Stella with this story which again she will neither confirm nor deny. The play ends on a close-up of her enigmatic smile.[5]

IV   *The Implications of* The Collection

Taylor, reviewing the stage production of this play, observed that it was a comedy that started off lightly enough but turned into "something much more uncomfortable and obsessional" than the average viewer or audience expected.[6] The title, presumably, refers to the Chinese vases (an excellent symbol for the fragile sexual relationship as we can see in Wycherley's *The Country Wife* or Pope's *The Rape of the Lock*), the collection of clothes shown at Leeds, but principally to the collection of "truths" the play displays. It is clearly not important whether or not Bill and Stella *did* sleep together in Leeds; what matters is the potential the idea of that act contains for liberating a large number of illusions which either strengthen or destroy the lives of four people. And the situation is given an extra twist because the quartet is not two couples but one woman and three men. In the action of the play Bill and Stella, who never meet (for such a meeting would be fatal) swap partners and then return to the status quo. So *The Collection* is not just a comedy of manners kept deliberately slight, as Taylor suggests. It is full of questions, it involves class warfare (which all good comedy of manners must), and it pushes the themes of menace, verification, and the sexual potential of a woman a stage further.

The menace is muted of course. James's terrorization of Bill is amiable and is partly welcomed by Bill who suddenly finds himself the center of interest, the subject of the attention of another, younger, man and accused of intercourse with that man's wife.

Verification is less important than the recognition that two relationships have gone stale, fallen into habit and have been jolted; all four people now have to rethink the basis of their relationships (or rather three have to since we can probably exclude the star of the play, Stella). This rethinking is reflected in small details, such as James's demand for olives (which he does not like) or Bill's declining potatoes with the Sunday roast (which he has always had). At the end James has returned to question Stella about her ambiguous role, but is getting no satisfactory answer. Because words cannot provide a satisfactory answer; only actions. Stella herself has a dual personality which James accepts: on the one hand she is a career woman, capable, independent and often away on business while on the other hand she appears in the play as totally passive; curled up on her couch silently fondling her kitten. Surprisingly no Freudian so far has translated kitten as pussy! There is an irony that to rouse her husband she has sent him off to form another possible attachment, but it is an irony she surely recognizes. Her husband will at least recognize the "truth" of his own sexuality as well as hers. If, that is, he is not too preoccupied with mere words, and demanding an answer to the question is my wife a whore? After the next play, *The Lover,* the conjunction of these two words, "wife" and "whore," is more obviously central though it pushes forward a topic discussed in Sally/Katina in *Night School* (who looks back to Virginia in *The Dwarfs*). In the first interview between James and Bill the two words are joined together, a hint that looks forward to *The Lover.*

Here, then, is a bedroom farce in which Pinter traces an ordinary story about getting at the truth. Esslin sees Stella as too passive; if she is the original bone of contention she is soon lost from sight and excluded from the male world. But this misses two points. First, it is not an exclusively male world since all three characters are probably bisexual (at least). Second, Stella has that great ability (in Pinterland, anyway) of knowing when to speak and when to keep silent—whatever the sexual nature of the three men it is her sexuality that keeps them all on the go; she need only be seen silent and stroking her kitten.

This play recalls the Coward of *Private Lives* in which the partners are restored at the end. And if it is an autumn play the collection shown will surely be for spring or summer. D. L. Hirst has suggested that if

Truth is a nebulous concept "one can reach some approximation of it by carefull attention to language, expression, style, tone of voice. Pinter reveals that people believe what they like and for them that becomes, indeed is, the truth." What matters is ones ability to respond to the role offered and sustain it; Stella's look at the end is friendly and sympathetic—James should recognize both sides of her as the truth. But his final question suggests failure.

Trussler finds these characters boring people, in "dramatised chess problems"; and he uses the word "mannered" to condemn the plays. They are mannered plays—what else could they be? To criticize them on this ground is to miss the point and also the fun.

V   The Lover

The Lover is obviously a television play from the first shot: bongo drums (an echo from *The Birthday Party?*) in close-up—lost, of course, in any stage production. The play, in fact, is full of details showing Pinter's fascination with technique—stage directions now contain phrases like "cut" and "shot" and other purely televisual instructions.

The setting of the play is spacious and luxurious—a house in the country, near Windsor, in high summer—which is in sharp contrast to shabby winter rooms in the town. The opening of the play is witty and startling:

RICHARD *(amiably)*:   Is your lover coming today?
SARAH: Mmnn.
RICHARD: What time?
SARAH: Three.
RICHARD: Will you be going out . . . or staying in?
SARAH: Oh . . . I think we'll stay in.
RICHARD: I thought you wanted to go to that exhibition?
SARAH: I did, yes . . . but I think I'd prefer to stay in with him today.
RICHARD: Mmn—hmmn. Well, I must be off.
SARAH: Mmnnn.
RICHARD: Will he be staying long do you think?
SARAH: Mmmnnn . . .
RICHARD: About . . . six, then?
SARAH: Yes.
RICHARD: Have a pleasant afternoon.
SARAH: Mmnn.

RICHARD: Bye-bye.
SARAH: Bye.

Sarah, who changes into high heels and a tight, black, "sexy dress,"
settles down to wait for her lover. The doorbell rings, and, as she opens
the door to him, the scene fades. Richard returns in the early evening,
and after posing polite questions about her afternoon and whether or
not it was pleasant, startles her by asking if she ever thinks of him,
working hard at the office while she is being unfaithful to him at home.
She replies that at certain moments she does think of him, but the picture is not terribly convincing. After changing her shoes (she has forgotten to remove the high-heeled shoes of the afternoon), she tells him
why. She points out that he is not working hard at the office, he is
spending the afternoon with his mistress. Richard admits to a whore,
but not a mistress—and to a whore, moreover, who lacks the grace,
elegance, and wit that Sarah assumes she has:

RICHARD   *(Laughing)*:   These terms just don't apply. You can't sensibly
            enquire whether a whore is witty. It's of no significance
            whether she is or she isn't. She's simply a whore, a functionary
            who either pleases or displeases.
SARAH: And she pleases you?
RICHARD: Today she is pleasing. Tomorrow . . .? One can't say.
(Pause)
SARAH: I must say I find your attitude to women rather alarming.
RICHARD: Why? I wasn't looking for a woman I could respect, as you,
            whom I could admire and love, as I do you. Was I? All I wanted
            was . . . how shall I put it . . . someone who could express and
            engender lust with all lust's cunning. Nothing more.[7]

    Such amusing if heartless dialogue reminds us of Restoration com-
edy and becomes serious only in the light of the information given us
at the end of the act. Asking questions about what Sarah does in the
afternoon is, apparently, not in the rules of the game and upsets Sarah.
She is reassured, however, that things are still "beautifully balanced."
She prepares for another afternoon.
    At this point Pinter introduces another character. When the doorbell
rings it is not Sarah's lover after all but John, the milkman, who offers
her (with whatever innuendo the reader may supply) cream. Sarah
declines. The next ring does, however, announce the arrival of her
lover, Richard, dressed casually in light slacks and a suede jacket. Sarah
calls him Max.

Act Two shows the games Max-Richard and Sarah play in the afternoon. Once more the camera focuses on passionate tapping on the bongo drums and then the two begin to play out their roles. First, Max is a lecherous stranger making advances to an unwilling Sarah; then Max is a kind park-keeper who rescues Sarah and then has to fight off her sexual advances until they both fall to the floor for the teatime game. These games, clearly defined by custom, are threatened when Max-Richard also starts asking questions. Max asks where her husband is and says that he must give her up because his wife does not know what he is doing:

MAX: No, she doesn't know. She thinks I know a whore, that's all. Some spare-time whore, that's all. That's what she thinks.
SARAH: Yes, but be sensible . . . my love . . . she doesn't mind, does she?
MAX: She'd mind if she knew that, in fact . . . I've got a full-time mistress, two or three times a week, a woman of grace, elegance, wit, imagination—
SARAH: Yes, yes, you have—
MAX: In an affair that's been going on for years.[8]

This line of argument from Max naturally surprises Sarah. Max says that he has played his last game; he must think of his wife and of the children who will soon be home from boarding school. And when Sarah tries to play the "teatime" game to distract him, he rejects her coolly on the grounds that she is too bony:

MAX: You're not plump enough. You're nowhere near plump enough. You know what I like. I like enormous women. Like bullocks with udders. Vast uddered bullocks.
SARAH: You mean cows.
MAX: I don't mean cows. I mean voluminous great uddered feminine bullocks. Once, years ago, you vaguely resembled one.
SARAH: Oh, thanks.
MAX: But now, quite honestly, compared to my ideal . . . you're skin and bone.
They stare at each other.
He puts on his jacket.
SARAH: You're having a lovely joke.
MAX: It's no joke.
He goes.[9]

When Richard returns from a tiring day at the office, he finds that Sarah's afternoon has not been a success. He is fairly sympathetic, but

he objects to a cold dinner, suggesting tartly that Sarah's afternoon pas-
times are beginning to interfere with her wifely duties. In answer to
Sarah's question about his whore's being bony he replies, confusingly,
that he likes thin women! Richard now begins a new game, namely, to
forbid Max entry to the house—Sarah may no longer receive him
there. He "discovers" the bongo drums and asks what their purpose is,
upsetting Sarah, who reminds him that the arrangement was simply no
questions asked. When Richard perseveres, she retaliates:

You paltry, stupid . . . ! Do you think he's the only one who comes! Do you?
Do you think he's the only one I entertain? Mmmnnn? Don't be silly. I have
other visitors, other visitors, all the time, I receive all the time. Other afternoons, all the time. When ñeither of you know, neither of you. I give them
strawberries in season. With cream. Strangers, total strangers. But not to me,
not while they're here. They come to see the hollyhocks. And then they stay
for tea. Always. Always.[10]

The scene with John, the milkman, in Act One suggests that this is
probably not true, but Richard-Max cannot be sure. At any rate, he
stops the new game and moves back into the park game. Gradually,
although dressed for the evening, the two slip into the sequence of
characters they assume in the afternoon until Richard tells Sarah to
change her clothes and calls her his lovely whore.

VI   *The Meaning of* The Lover

It comes as no surprise to find Trussler unsympathetic to this play,
which he dismisses as anecdotal "and once one knows the punch-line
of the anecdote there's not a lot of interest left."[11] Other critics, too,
have worried about the reality of those children, for example (usually
with Albee's play *Who's Afraid of Virginia Woolf?* in mind). At the
opening of the play the couple sound like Elyot and Amanda but the
coup de théâtre which closes the first act revealing the lover (husband)
throws all the previous dialogue into a new perspective just as it puts
the subsequent games into another light. There is an obvious streak of
sado-masochism in the games but that should not be considered too
unusual. As Anthony Storr points out in his study, *Sexual Deviations:*

It is only when sado-masochism is extreme or divorced from sexual intercourse that it can be accounted a deviation. For countless couples engage in
minor sado-masochistic rituals which serve the purpose of arousing them erot-
ically, and are thus valuable introductory steps to the sexual act itself.[12]

The interest in this play lies in the fact that instead of two couples, as in *The Collection,* Pinter achieves his four characters by splitting up one couple. The games played are elaborate and clearly ritualistic; they separate the respectable husband-wife relationship from the more passionate lover-mistress/whore relationship. Within the alternative relationship the roles can change rapidly from dominant to dominated, from modesty to shameless immodesty. The pattern seems so established that it implies long duration, habit, so that it is not surprising that Sarah and Richard have begun to act as though they were being unfaithful and show jealousy of their alter egoes. Nor is it surprising that the games no longer function vitally and that Richard, at least, wants a change.

The play invited comparison, immediately, with Osborne's *Under Plain Cover* (the second of the *Plays for England*) but, as Taylor observes, Pinter's treatment is deeper: "It is not just a game for keeping marriage fresh and exciting, but an acceptance of the inescapable fact that each person is 'the sum of so many reflections.' . . . And it all amounts to a successfully working marriage of ten years' standing, with children (at boarding school) and no outside involvements."[13] We had better ignore those children and indeed all demands for more information, more background (what, for example, is the source of their income since Richard is hardly ever at work?). Osborne's wife and husband have two children who are actually brought onstage, but then the Osborne play becomes less concerned with games young couples play and more concerned with the fact that they are innocently incestuous which allows the play to shift into a diatribe against the press which intrudes in the name of the public. *Under Plain Cover* buckles under the pressure of Osborne's private vendetta with the press and turns into the cheaply sensational kind of story it pretends to deplore. The games in *Under Plain Cover* are also more physically perverse involving, as the title suggests, a great deal of equipment. However if we take the children (and ten years) seriously we can understand why the time has come to take stock of a situation that has become as stale as the original situation it was to keep alive; perhaps, Richard suggests, Max could come to dinner?

Baker/Tabachnik take a pessimistic view of the ending assuming that the dream life has taken over completely, which illustrates the dangers of fantasy. They are certainly in the wrong clothes at the end of the play but then that itself illustrates a shift. And as usual the play ends on a question to be answered by the audience. Here the dramatist is superior to a critic who is expected to give an answer in the end and may, like James in *The Collection,* be asking the wrong question. Esslin compares the play to *The Bacchae,* albeit in miniature, and its subject is the conflict between "tamed, socialized and wild, instinct dominated humanity,"[14] but of course a comparison with any Restoration comedy would do as well.

At the end of the play it is not even a question of trying to bring the two rituals together, incorporating the respectable wife in the sexy whore, the staid husband and the saturnine lover; it is surely a matter of accepting that Max and his whore are as real as Sarah and Richard who play them and perhaps now they no longer need fancy dress and bongo drums. Richard's demand for a feminine bullock suggests that he wants Sarah's urges to be as strong as his, unhampered by the labels of woman and wife and mother.

VII   *Criticism of* The Lover

The critics who saw the stage production of *The Lover* seemed baffled. Perhaps the fact that it was coupled with *The Dwarfs* partly explains their bafflement. It remained for the reviewer in *The Financial Times* to treat the play seriously, connect it with *Under Plain Cover* but also note how important the wit and elegance were, conferring upon the situation what Osborne could not: "For, where Mr. Osborne is a moralist who must give rein to his indignation, Mr. Pinter is an analyst and stylist. Mr. Osborne rails at life, Mr. Pinter notes its patterns and arranges it." Harold Hobson, in *The Sunday Times,* cited the medieval *cours d'amour* where it was publically debated which of the two was better—husband or lover, which is not really much help. Only Bamber Gascoigne, in the *Observer,* looked at the structure of the play pointing out that Act Two destroys (I would suggest qualifies) what had gone before, making two plays, of which the second gradually develops a new theme on a different level. But the acts are not separate; indeed they are nearly the same act repeated but from another point of view; which, since this is Pinter, not Conrad, is the same, only different.

CHAPTER 6

The Homecoming

BETWEEN 1960 and 1965 Pinter was not particularly active in the theater. Including the rejected play *Night School* he wrote only three short plays for television; three or four more sketches, including a special cricket sketch performed by Pinter and Pleasance at a charity show given by the Lord Taverners; and a short story. The new sketches, presented by Michael Bakewell on the BBC Third Program, consisted of "Applicant," already published; "Dialogue for Three," published in *Stand* magazine; and three sketches: "That's All," "That's Your Trouble," and "Interview." In "That's All," Mrs. A and Mrs. B discuss the day on which they and a third woman visit the butcher and afterwards make a cup of tea; in "That's Your Trouble," two men-about town discuss in a park the strains imposed upon a man who is carrying a sandwich-board; and in "Interview," Mr. Jakes (that is, a privy?) is interviewed about trade in his pornographic bookshops. As Bakewell commented in the *Radio Times*, the sketches show Pinter working in miniature, "with all his remarkable feeling for the subtleties, manners and banalities of speech and action."

I *"Tea Party"*

Pinter read his short story "Tea Party" on the BBC Third Program in 1964 and later published it in *Playboy* magazine. It has now been reprinted in *Poems and Prose: 1949–77*, where Pinter says that it was written in 1963 and is, he believes, more successful than the later play version. It is a story about a man whose suspicions concerning his wife, sons, brother-in-law, and secretary induce periods of blindness during which he loses his grip on reality and finds his skills and abilities being slowly destroyed. In its use of blindness, various kinds of weather, and the loss of skills, it is strongly reminiscent of *A Slight Ache*, as are the social and sexual implications. A man—with a wife, two sons, his

brother-in-law as a business partner, and a perfect secretary—who has
been successful in business, in making love, at carpentry, and at ping-
pong is waiting for his doctor to remove the bandages from his eyes.
As he reflects on his relationships with these people and his failing
abilities, he feels that friends and relations are all, in some way, deceiv-
ing him, and that his wife is being seduced. But he concludes that such
things could not, surely, happen at a tea party with all his family present? The story provides an interesting comparison with A *Slight Ache;*
it also illustrates the notions raised by Freud in his paper "Those
Wrecked by Success."[1]

II Tea Party

The short story (with an epigraph from H. G. Wells—"In the country of the blind he found himself a king") was the basis for a television
play, produced on March 25, 1965. Commissioned by the European
Broadcasting Union for "The Largest Theater in the World" and lasting seventy-five minutes, *Tea Party* appeared simultaneously in
France, Belgium, Luxembourg, Switzerland, Germany, Austria, Spain,
Holland, Denmark, Sweden, Norway, and Britain; Italy refused to
show it. It took a month to write and Pinter described it in the *Daily
Mirror* (March 26, 1965) as "the story of a businessman's reaction to
his new secretary and the effect she has on him. He hires her on the
day before his marriage." Pinter later described the play as cinematic:
"I wrote it like that. Television and films are simpler than the theater—
if you get tired of a scene you just drop it and go on to another one.
(I'm exaggerating of course.) What *is* so different about the stage is
that you're just *there,* stuck—there are your characters stuck on the
stage, you've got to live with them and deal with them."[2]

This version of "Tea Party" is about a self-made business man, Robert Disson, who from humble beginnings, has become the head of one
of the largest sanitary engineering firms in the country. He hires a new
secretary, marries for a second time and finds that he cannot, literally,
believe his eyes. The original story has been expanded: the ubiquitous
spectacles are not in the television play; cryptic details in the story are
filled out and relationships are made more precise. Disson's downfall
is more concrete in the play than in the story: he collapses into a catatonic trance. The division between reality and fantasy is made clearer
without destroying the equivocal nature of the experience and more is
made of the social backgrounds from which the dilemma partly

springs. The play is Pinter's first family play, though it is, of course, the second party organized to destroy the guest of honor! It was also interesting to see how completely the visual appeal, the camera work, illumined the dialogue. The critics treated the play respectfully. Mary Crozier, in the *Guardian*, Eric Shorter, in the *Daily Telegraph*, and Maurice Wiggin, in *The Sunday Times*, liked the play in various ways; on the other hand Maurice Richardson, in the *Observer*, found it clever but "a simple, rather shallow piece." Patrick Anderson, in the *Spectator* (April 2, 1965), saw the appropriateness of Disson's purging society of its waste products and his inability to purge the subconscious but he felt the play was too much of a case history, a view partially supported by John Holstrom, in the *New Statesman*, who thought the play "intriguing, funny in parts, sexy in parts, never entirely satisfactory." No one was perhaps as precise and detailed as the anonymous critic of *The Times* (March 26, 1965) who pointed out that we once more had a play about a sanctuary—the vast modern office building barricaded by wealth and power but resting on plumbing—and a hero still beset by some obscure dread. The long deserted corridors, the locked offices, and the former self of Disson exact revenges for his success. He marries a politician's daughter, engages her brother in his business, but is attacked by doubts and blindness. He finally collapses at the office tea party and retreats into a catatonic trance, the most complete sanctuary. This critic also noted the use of fetishes—leather, high heels—and saw the play as a game of mutual provocation between Disson and his secretary, defying the icily dehumanized setting.

Tea Party was shown only once, which makes the critics' task difficult. Certain ideas emerge, however. After Disley warns the guests that Disson's eyes are strained but that they must not embarrass him by speaking of it, the play was divided, visually, into two kinds of shots: Disson's point of view (what he thinks is happening) and shots that include Disson (what is, presumably, happening). Since both are filmed they must both be happening, of course! Disson's point of view was soundless action, reflecting the tensions that have been built up in the play, but other shots show the normal, if strained atmosphere of a tea party. When Disson "sees" Willy pile cushions on Wendy's desk and help both Wendy and Diana onto them and then "sees" Willy begin to caress them, he collapses and hears nothing—not even Diana's closing words: ". . . It's your wife." The play ends on a close-up of Disson's open but unseeing eyes.

This ending, as the critic in the *Listener* (April 15, 1965) observed, is the crisis of the play and could have been the beginning of another. But it is unlikely that a dramatist would try to send an audience out of a theater at such a moment. If we read this final collapse as a kind of death totally unexpected by innocent bystanders, then it forms a conventional sort of ending, though without the conventional restoration of order. We can suggest certain "explanations" of the play. Disson marries above himself to stabilize his place in upper-class society. But his real character shows itself with Wendy—his behavior as he himself says, is something that only takes place in paperback books, not in life. Class warfare, success, relationships that collapse, all center on a hero who tries to conceal them in more trivial failures—an inability to play ping-pong or do woodwork. But eventually his suspicions, jealousy, and fear of inadequacy reduce him to the condition forced on Edward in *A Slight Ache*. The reasons may be different, though it is noticeable that Edward married the squire's daughter in order to rise in the world. But in *Tea Party* for the first time relationships are examined in the context of a family, a family of several generations which looks forward to *The Homecoming*. The number of characters, however, remains small. And as in all his television plays from *A Night Out* onward, sex is firmly established as part of Pinterland. Disson becomes suspicious of every relationship: with his best friend (in the story nothing so precise as gastric flu accounts for his inability to attend the wedding, nor is it specified that his best man and physician are the same); with his wife, whom he cannot really believe wants to marry him and whom he suspects of having too close a relationship with her brother (the remark about playing brother and sister at Sunderley is both ambiguous and sinister); with his twin sons who, always polite, seem to mock and menace him more and more as the play proceeds; and with Wendy, with whom his game is played in the dark and whom he suspects of being unfaithful to him with Willy. Even Diana and Wendy are suspected of having a particular relationship in one scene.

In this world of the successful, the well-bred, and the self-made, sickness and isolation remain the problem. Curiously the more family there is, and the more success there is, the more isolated and suspicious Disson seems to be. The play covers a longer period of time than is usual— one year—with no precise indications of how rapidly the breakdown takes place. This development could have been more clearly indicated, since a short play is presenting a long, slow process, perhaps too rapidly for an audience's credulity. The blindness itself—a blank screen flecked with gray-white patches—captures the feelings of Disson very well; just as close-ups suggest isolation by cutting everything else out, underlining the tensions and insecurity. The symbolic objects—water closets, bidets, Ping-Pong ball, and mirrors work alongside shots of fetishist objects (leather, black chiffon, high heels) and are incorporated in scenes like the football game with the table lighter (which at one point lay at Wendy's feet like an apple!) or a game of chess, giving the play a brilliant but evasive surface and suggesting that we cannot be entirely sure that the whole thing is not a nasty dream of Disson's guilty, secret, true self.

Surprisingly *Tea Party* has been staged, in 1968 at the East-side Playhouse in New York, and in London, in 1970 at the Duchess Theatre. On both occasions the director, James Hammerstein, coupled *Tea Party* with another translation from television, *The Basement*. If not major Pinter, Taylor, in *Plays and Players* (November 1970), found them satisfying as comic variations on familiar themes and, more importantly, stepping stones between *The Lover* and *The Homecoming*.

III   The Basement

This play was written as a film scenario, as part of a trilogy with Beckett and Ionesco. It was originally called *The Compartment*, but neither it nor Ionesco's *The Hard-Boiled Egg* was actually filmed, though Beckett's *Film*, with Buster Keaton, was made into a movie short. Perhaps the context of the scenario suggested some of the treatment by Pinter for it reads as one of his most symbolic works. Perhaps symbolic is misleading. The constant alternation of summer and winter, day and night, hot and cold, may serve only to indicate the passage of time. The subject of the play draws on "Kullus" (1949) and "The Examination" (1958); there are three people and a room. Much of the action is pictorial, even more so than *Tea Party*, and the action resembles a dream. Indeed Esslin has suggested that the realistic basis for the film may be no more than the initial shot of Law sitting by the fire trying to read his book.[3] The film opens on a dark night outside. Stott, in a raincoat, and Jane are looking at the light shining out from a basement flat. Inside, in a warm, lighted, comfortable room, Tim Law sits by the fire reading. When the bell rings, he answers it, greets Stott affectionately, taking off his coat, producing a towel and slippers, and offers a drink, or coffee, and a bed for the night. His hospitality is only partly checked when Stott says he has a friend with him and asks if she may come in, too. Jane enters, and as Stott starts putting out the lights, she climbs into bed, where Stott joins her. Tim settles down by the one shaded lamp, and while Stott and Jane make love, continues to read an illustrated edition of a Persian love manual. Apparently Tim has shared a flat previously with Stott and remembers the relationship with pleasure. Although his present flat is more comfortable, and although he insists that he is happy, he admits that he sometimes gets lonely living alone.

The scene shifts to a beach on a summer's day. Jane is making sandcastles, and Tim is talking to Stott who is, according to Tim, a brilliant Sanskrit scholar and connected with the French aristocracy. At night, after Stott and Jane have made love, she leans over and smiles at Tim.

Stott now begins to change the room, first removing the pictures and finally replacing the furniture with modern Scandinavian furniture—only the bed and the curtains remain unchanged. With Jane as spectator, Stott and Tim run a race, but, when Stott does not run, Tim looks back and falls. At this point Tim suggests that three in one room are a bit of a crowd. However, Stott is perfectly happy. In the next scene on the beach, Jane is trying to get rid of Stott so that she and Tim can live comfortably together, but Tim tells Stott of Jane's intention and protests that she is dirtying the clean Scandinavian furniture. Stott apparently falls ill and nearly dies, but he convalesces in a room now decorated in the grand Italian manner, with Tim playing a flute. Throwing marbles at him, Stott hits him in the face, and after Tim has shattered a goldfish tank with a marble, Stott knocks him down with a marble aimed at his head.

While Jane is making instant coffee in the kitchen, Stott and Tim, in a completely bare room, advance on each other with broken milk bottles in hand. They parry and smash together. The camera moves to the first shot of a cold, wet, dark exterior where Tim, wearing Stott's raincoat, and Jane huddled once more against the wall, are looking at the light coming from a basement flat. Inside the room is furnished as it was at the beginning and Stott is reading comfortably by the fire. When the bell rings, he opens the door and greets Tim enthusiastically. The question remains as to whether or not Stott will invite Jane in and begin the action again.

The play is full of Pinter motifs. Some sort of strong relationship between the two men seems to exist which is challenged by the arrival of a girl. Baker/Tabchnik interpret the play as follows:

Law reveals a concern with law. His worry about Jane's dirtying and sullying of the room reflects the obsessiveness of the superego. Stott, on the other hand, has a name that suggests an animal that bores, for instance "stoat." Like the luxury-loving id, Stott has yachts, cars, paintings, money. In their trading off of Jane, the men represent the forces of superego and id, respectively, contending for dominance in the "basement" of the subconscious mind. Sometimes one is victorious, and sometimes the other. Jane serves . . . as both catalyst and object of the men's needs, a colorless role . . . to which men relegate women, according to Pinter.[4]

How was a compartment different from a room? When the play was televised by the BBC on February 20, 1967, Pinter, who played the role of Stott, had changed the title simply to *The Basement* which suggested a Freudian interpretation for the basement is "the lower depths of the house, . . . where lust lives in the unconscious. The upper house, the conscious mind, is dark, asleep. Thus the setting and the title provide the hint that this play is truly a dream, a dream of lust "in which, moreover, a son fights the father for a promiscuous mother.[5] Which some see as the subject of *The Homecoming*. But noticeably the female plays a very passive part here (her name, perhaps, is taken from the Tarzan stories?), unlike the female in *The Homecoming*. And if the changes of weather and furnishings in the flat reflect the passage of time they also seem to reflect the changing emotional relationship of the three characters.

IV   The Homecoming

The night after the BBC production of *Tea Party*, the Royal Shakespeare Company presented, in Cardiff, Pinter's *The Homecoming*, which, after a short provincial tour, entered the repertory at the Aldwych in June 1965. Directed by Peter Hall, the cast included Vivien Merchant in the role of Ruth. Many consider it to be his finest play, so far, although Trussler, not surprisingly, is incredulous "at the aimlessness of plot and arbitrariness of feeling alike."[6] Pinter feels that it is the "only play which gets remotely near to a structural entity which satisfies me. . . . *The Birthday Party* and *The Caretaker* have too much writing. . . . I want to iron it down, eliminate things. Too many words irritate me sometimes, but I can't blame them, they just seem to come out—out of the fellow's mouth."[7] The plot was inspired by a boyhood friend from Hackney who went to Canada to teach and get secretly married before returning home to surprise his family,[8] and in this play Pinter comes out into the open. The play deals with the tensions in a Jewish family, and Baker/Tabachnik see it as an exorcism. After *The Homecoming* "Pinter could walk out of the mental prison of Hackney and the East End a free man."[9] The clue, apparently, is the name Ruth, who was the Moabite mistress of King David—so the family is Jewish and Ruth is not, a theme, according to Charles Spencer, "close to the author's experience, since he married a non-Jewess, before fame and success, and no doubt had to face a typical Jewish reaction."[10] Perhaps—but the situation remains universal and the "freedom" is limited by memory, as subsequent plays demonstrate.

V   *The Action of* The Homecoming

The Homecoming is a summer play that belies its weather. Set in an old Victorian house in north London, the play is a series of bouts in a battle that is mainly verbal but which occasionally takes the form of physical violence. Each member of the family looks to his own advantage, using what weapons—cunning, virility, intelligence, or sex—he or she possesses. The opening scene is between a taciturn Lenny (he is trying to read a newspaper) and his aggressively talkative father, Max. Their relationship is suggested in the following exchange:

LENNY: Plug it, will you, you stupid sod, I'm trying to read the paper.
MAX: Listen? I'll chop your spine off, you talk to me like that! You understand? Talking to your lousy filthy father like that!
LENNY: You know what, you're getting demented.

Max, stimulated by a query about horse-racing put forward by Lenny just to annoy him, romances (or tells the "truth") about the time when he was young, a rebel, with his friend MacGregor, and about the way he had with horses, denied fulfillment because of family obligations. When Lenny taunts him, Max raises his stick, but Lenny only mocks the gesture with a little boy's voice. The arrival of Sam shifts the focus of attack. Lenny quietly "sends up" his uncle by harping on his qualities of politeness, courtesy, and efficiency as a driver and excludes Max from the conversation, thus achieving the maximum amount of irritation at the expense of both his father and his uncle. When Lenny tires of the game he leaves, and Max immediately starts to sneer at Sam's gifts, which have not included women and virility but which do include niceness, a conventional attitude to women, marriage, and life in general. This episode is ended by the arrival of another son, Joey, whose innocent remark that he is hungry goads Max into a bitter diatribe about the mess he finds himself in. When Joey tactfully goes upstairs Max returns to his attack on Sam. Sam insists on speaking well of Max's late wife, Jessie, whom he characterizes as a perfect lady, but he damns Max's friend MacGregor in a brutal, brisk fashion. Max turns savagely on him and threatens to throw him out of the house when he ceases to be economically useful, but Sam counters by reminding him that it is their mother's house, their father's house, and the scene ends with Max's bitter reminiscences about his father.

Scene 2 introduces the eldest son, Teddy, who, with his wife, Ruth, is returning from abroad very early in the morning. From the beginning they are a familiar Pinter couple, at odds with each other. They disagree on simple matters such as staying with the family or not and staying up or going to bed; they change attitudes without knowing why and Teddy seems unduly insistent that Ruth should not be afraid of his family, who are nice, warm people. Ruth goes out for a walk and Lenny enters. However, after six years' separation, the two brothers have nothing more to talk about than Lenny's insomnia and the tick of his clock; and, as Teddy goes to bed, he declines a glass of water offered by his hospitable brother. Ruth returns, and she also discusses Lenny's tick, Venice (where they have just been), the difference in things between day and night—all in an interested if inconsequential manner—until Lenny gives her a glass of water and asks if he can touch her. When Ruth asks why she is told a long story about a society lady who took liberties with Lenny down by the docks and got kicked because he had decided she was diseased. Lenny's sensitivity, which the story is to illustrate, is confirmed in a further anecdote concerning an old lady and her mangle. She, too, was beaten up by Lenny.

Lenny, having established his power over women, challenges Ruth by moving the ashtray (which she is not using) and than by trying to take away her glass, but she counterattacks, making suggestions to him which alarm him. She finishes her drink and goes to bed, leaving Lenny trying to figure out what sort of a proposal she has just made him. He does this so noisily that he awakens Max, who comes down and wants to know whom he is hiding. This demand for an explanation is countered by Lenny's asking for information about the night of his conception. Was he intended or accidental? Since Max is silent, Lenny muses on why he did not ask his dear mother, at the mention of whom

Max spits at him, and the scene ends with a joke about having to vacuum the carpet.

Scene 3 is after breakfast in the early morning. Joey is doing push-
ups in front of the mirror. Max, curiously resentful of Sam, who is
washing up in the kitchen, finally calls him in and attacks him for har-
boring resentment against Max! The usual complaints against Sam are
listed—his lack of violence and greed—and only the arrival of Teddy
and Ruth in dressing gowns ends this episode. Max feels a fool because
his son has returned so casually and attacks Ruth, calling her a dirty
tart and a filthy scrubber, finally telling Joey to throw her out. Joey,
however, merely reminds Max that he is an old man and is promptly
punched in the belly for saying so. The effort of doing this overwhelms
Max, but as Sam hurries forward to help him Max hits Sam over the
head with his stick and sinks, breathless, onto the couch. Suddenly Max
addresses Ruth normally, asking her if she has any children, greets
Teddy with great affection, inviting him to kiss and cuddle his father.
Teddy accepts, and the act ends with Max's declaration that Teddy
still loves his father. This sentimentalism seems characteristically Jewish, yet nowhere in the play is it insisted upon that the family is Jewish.
It should also be noted that this sentimentality is as ironic and savage
as anything else in the play. Teddy, in fact, means to punch his father
if he were to come for that kiss and cuddle!

Act Two opens with a long tableau of the family assembled for
lunch. Max leers charmingly at Ruth, who compliments him on lunch.
He compliments her on the coffee and, in this saccharine atmosphere
of *bonhomie*, he grows nostalgic, regretting that Jessie and the grandchildren (Teddy's sons in America) are not there so that she could make
a fuss over them. He talks nostalgically of an episode in his own life
with Jessie and their sons but this charming family idyll is rapidly
replaced by a brutal and succinct account of a crippled family, three
bastard sons, and a bitch of a wife. In this more customary vein, Max
returns to insulting Sam on the usual grounds—weakness, lack of virility (that is, violence), and idleness. Sam, insulted, leaves for work, after
first shaking hands with Ruth courteously. Max then starts a conversation about Ruth as a good cook and a good wife, and gives Ruth and
Teddy, rather belatedly, his blessing. Teddy supports this gracious picture of Ruth by describing their happy life in America in a successful
department in a flourishing university—a picture Ruth immediately
qualifies with the suggestion, hesitant but clear, that she was different
before she met Teddy. Teddy's too hasty rejection of this qualification
produces a tension apparently relieved by Lenny's discussion of phi-

losophy. The philosophical inquiry—into the nature of a table (in order to bait Teddy, whose Ph.D. is, surprisingly, in philosophy) and what to do with it when one has taken it—is dissolving into laughter because of the suggestions of Max (sell it) and Joey (chop it up for firewood) when Ruth alters the tone by substituting her leg and underwear for the table as an object for consideration. This reminder of her physical attractiveness, coupled with her view of America as all rocks and insects, produces another embarrassed silence. And the family leaves in a quiet, brisk, but orderly manner.

It is now Teddy, not Ruth, who wishes to go straight back to America, pushing the claims of his own family and reminding us that there are two families—his family here (father, uncle, brothers) and his family in America (three sons). He contrasts the cleanness of America with the dirt of north London. When he leaves to pack, Lenny enters, discussing the change in the weather and the need for new winter clothes. Ruth once more focuses attention on her body by asking him to admire her shoes (and, incidentally, her legs). She tells him of her life as a photographer's model before she married Teddy and how she used to go to the country to a large house with a lake. She describes how she went there before she left for America with Teddy, saw the house brilliant with light, but she was shut out. Teddy returns with her coat and the suitcases, but she accepts Lenny's offer to dance, and she is kissing him when Joey and Max return. As Joey remarks, Teddy has married a tart, and to prove it, he takes over from Lenny, lying on top of her on the couch while Lenny strokes her hair. Max unconcernedly discusses Teddy's departure and Ruth as a woman of feeling. Teddy says and does nothing. Abruptly the mood changes. Ruth, by now on the floor with Joey, pushes him aside and asks for food and drink. She insists on having her whiskey in a tumbler and, suddenly, attacks Teddy on the subject of his critical works which the family have never seen and would not, according to Teddy, understand:

You're just objects. You just . . . move about. I can observe it. I can see what you do. It's the same as I do. But you're lost in it. You won't get me being . . . I won't be lost in it.[11]

An attack by the family on Teddy's selfishness and lack of family feeling moves easily into an attack on the American way of life by Lenny, who appeals for grace, generosity of mind, and liberality of spirit!

At this point Joey, who has been upstairs with Ruth during Lenny's attack, comes down and the men discuss whether or not Ruth is a tease. Anecdotes are told to illustrate Joey's attractiveness for girls, but Teddy remains unmoved. Even when the family decides that it would like to keep Ruth and set her up as a prostitute, he remains unconcerned. He is moved neither to anger nor action when Lenny suggests that he should pimp for them in America, although he does decline to support Ruth if she stays. Sam's reminder that Teddy and Ruth are married is ignored.

When Ruth comes down it is Teddy who explains the plan to her. She considers it and then accepts it, but on her own terms, which show her as shrewd on the economic angle as Lenny. Sam's intervention, revealing that Jessie had been unfaithful with MacGregor, is brushed aside as the product of a diseased imagination and his collapse on to the floor ignored. Teddy is moved, but only to regret that Sam cannot now drive him to the airport, and after discussing various alternative methods of getting there with his father he leaves, with Ruth's parting injunction not to become a stranger in his ears.

The family now moves into the final tableau as Joey lies with his head on Ruth's lap. Max, after hinting that she will use them, drops his stick and crawls to her, protesting that he is not old and asking for a kiss. Lenny looks on, enigmatically aloof. This final tableau is one of a mother with her children. Ruth has, in fact, come home—or found it amidst the alien corn. The lack of sympathy for conventional goodness or morality suggests they would not be at home here. Respectable life is an illusion: inside the room dreams are violent, savage, cruel, sexual, and powerful. Ruth has come home to the family she merits and which deserves her; with or without moral overtones she is where, for the moment, she belongs.

VI   *Criticism of* The Homecoming

When the play opened in London reviewers were respectful if not entirely enthusiastic. The *Guardian* (June 5, 1965) said that the play was perfectly turned, but to what end? This was a view shared by other critics. David Benedictus, in the *Spectator* (June 11), read the play as autobiography: Teddy (= Pinter away from the stage for six years) with his wife (= work) returns to his family (= his public) and, he concluded, had not come home. Probably the most interesting critique came from Stuart Hall, in *Encore* (July-August 1965), where he observed that what keeps this family going is a constant sense of threat sustained by verbal assaults. The twist to the play is not Teddy's defeat but Ruth's betrayal. Hall found Teddy's long speech important: what he proposes may be virtues, but only in another setting. Teddy goes in for linguistic indulgence and, while he is modifying verbs, Joey and Lenny are operating on and with Ruth. The family needs a woman and gets one. Hall sees the whole play as exposing the machinery of fantasy, and Teddy loses because his fantasies are remote.

If most critics were respectful they were all troubled on one point— the apparent lack of moral content. Where could Pinter go after this black fable? And it is a fable; it would be hard to imagine a play that violates so many pieties and upsets so many scruples with so little interest in making itself credible. Although Esslin insists that the play can stand up "to the most meticulous examination as a piece of realistic theater"[12] he also interprets it as Oedipal dreams. Thus he has the best of both worlds, which is all right for a dramatist but looks shifty in a critic. Consideration of the play falls into three parts, each of which might provide a key: the family, the morality, and the philosophy.

VII *The Family*

Everybody has his own room in this house but the family meets in the living room, the back wall of which has been knocked down to give them more space, or turn the living room into a hall. This architectural change (which may stem from Pinter's dislike of a split set) took place when Jessie died, which suggests that the two events may be connected: that the loss of Jessie radically altered the family unit. In spite of family ties relationships throughout the play are strained, giving the impression that the "family" is a group of individuals constrained to live together as a unit by the simple fact that they are labeled a family. They live in their own rooms and fight in the hall.

Obviously, familiar Pinter themes spring to mind: possession of a room, dangers of communication, subterranean violence, intruding forces, and women who are simultaneously mother, wife, and whore. This is the first family Pinter has put on the stage, although he has suggested a large family in *Tea Party*, where the pieties that word evokes (and the title) contradict the action as experienced by the narrator. The same contradiction between what we expect from the title and a family and what we (not just the narrator) actually see gives impetus to the play. *The Homecoming* takes in four generations if we include absent grandparents and absent grandchildren, but it is not a play about the difference between generations. Rather it concerns the bonds that separate or unite what is conventionally held up to be a valuable relationship. The alien force (suggested by America and Teddy's Ph.D.) is in fact at home: Teddy, who has gotten out of the room, cannot resist coming back, and Ruth already belongs to the district and the class.

Sam and Max, as brothers, seem curiously unalike. Certainly no relationship exists between them as between the brothers in *The Caretaker*. Yet, again, they may be faces of the same character. Max is domineering, lecherous, aggressive, and contemptuous of Sam, who seems virtuous if ineffectual. Only as the play proceeds does Sam begin to emerge as an equally dubious character. His attitude toward women, and particularly toward Jessie, whom he admired, but from a distance, is contradicted by the "facts" as he knows them—or as the play presents women. Jessie was apparently unfaithful while Ruth is a tease and/or nymphomaniac. The women in the various anecdotes enlarge upon the picture presented by Aston in *The Caretaker*—diseased, domineering, or simply vehicles for lust (the society woman, the old lady with her mangle, and the "birds" at the Scrubs).

Sam's conventional reminder, when Max threatens to throw him out as soon as he ceases to be economically useful, that they are brothers in their father's house only produces an ambivalent memory of the father: "Our father? I remember him. Don't worry. You kid yourself. He used to come over to me and look down at me. My old man did. He'd bend right over me, then he'd pick me up. I was only that big. Then he'd dandle me. Give me the bottle, wipe me clean. Give me a smile. Pat me on the bum. Catch me coming down. I remember my father."[13] Yet when it suits Max (for example, when he is attacking Sam) he can evoke the sacred memory: "I respected my father not only as a man but as a number one butcher! And to prove it I followed him into the shop, I learned to carve a carcase at his knee. I commemorated his name in blood. I gave birth to three grown men! All on my own bat. What have you done?"[14]

In Act Two he remembers the family after his father's death: when he had to look after his bedridden mother and his invalid brothers, who needed psychiatrists. Which poses the question, what happened to the other brothers? It also suggests the conflict between his *family* and *his* family.

His family is Jessie and three sons who also exist as the occasion requires. Jessie is both a sacred memory and a whore. Max's first reference to her is symptomatic: "Mind you, she wasn't such a bad woman. Even though it made me sick just to look at her rotten stinking face she wasn't such a bad bitch. I gave her the best bleeding years of my life, anyway."[15] Since in the next breath he reminds Lenny that he is his "lousy filthy father" we have to judge how far the dialogue is badinage or gives something away. Max maintains during his long monologue on horses that family obligations prevented him from becoming a ducal trainer, but it is probable that his association with horses was limited to their meat—particularly in the light of those Continental butchers. He apparently suspects MacGregor and Jessie, but when Sam confirms that suspicion his statement is brushed aside as the product of a diseased imagination. Yet when Sam eulogizes Jessie's qualities as a lady and companion Max's only response is a quiet but exasperated "Christ!" When Joey asks for food and Max sarcastically asks if he is their mother he is attacking Joey, but he is also reflecting his frustration with the role of housekeeper.

His relationship with his sons is full of tension and ambivalence, as are his memories of parents and wife. We are told, in a savage passage, that Max loved to tuck the boys into bed and, later, what fun it was to give them baths. The first act ends with the embarrassing invitation to Teddy to have a kiss and cuddle, which clearly reflects what happened or what Max thinks ought to have happened. But his attacks on Joey as a useless boxer and his anger when Lenny calls him "Dad" several times reflect more contradictions in the play. When Teddy arrives he is obviously uneasy about introducing his wife to the family, which is ignorant, after six years, of the fact that he is married and has fathered three sons. He wants to slip into his old room and postpone the meeting until later. Why is not clear, though having seen the family it is understandable. But his real problem is his relationship with Ruth. When he and Lenny meet they have nothing to talk about except the tick of Lenny's clock. And why, we wonder, is Lenny so upset when Ruth, later, calls him Leonard, the name his mother gave him? Lenny does not tell his father that the prodigal has returned, with a wife. Instead he asks his father why he was born. He wants to know whether he was intended or accidental: a distinction that the label "family" overlooks:

I'm only asking this in a spirit of enquiry, you understand that, don't you? I'm curious. And there's lots of people of my age share that curiosity, you know that, Dad? They often ruminate, sometimes singly, sometimes in groups, about the true facts of that particular night—the night they were made in the image of those two people *at it.* It's a question long overdue, from my point of view, but as we happen to be passing the time of day here tonight I thought I'd pop it to you.[16]

The mention of Jessie only makes Max spit at Lenny.

Max's anger at not knowing about Teddy's return is understandable, particularly if Max suspects that Lenny has concealed the fact from him, but it does not explain the line that anger takes, accusing Ruth of being a dirty tart; nor the ironies of his confused syntax: "I've never had a whore under this roof before. Ever since your mother died. My word of honour. (To JOEY) Have you ever had a whore here? Has Lenny ever had a whore here? They come back from America, they bring this slopbucket with them. They bring the bedpan with them. (To TEDDY.) Take that disease away from me. Get her away from me."[17] But Max is old; for the young men Ruth has attractions that are not entirely maternal.

The second act shows the family gathered after lunch arranged like a Victorian photograph and exhibiting the pieties such a photograph was intended to celebrate—whatever the reality behind the picture was. This cozy assembly leads to nostalgic memories on Max's part about Jessie, who was, according to Max, the backbone of the family and who taught the boys all the morality they know, which, under the circumstances, is an ambiguous compliment. He pursues this idyllic picture to recall the night he entered a business association with a group of butchers and pampered Jessie and the boys: "I remember the boys came down, in their pyjamas, all their hair shining, their faces pink, it was before they started shaving, and they knelt down at our feet, Jessie's and mine. I tell you it was like Christmas."[18] But the boys have started shaving (that is, grown up), Max is old, and Ruth, anyway, punctures the dream with a question about the butchers, who, not unexpectedly, turned out to be a bunch of criminals. And the picture shifts rapidly to Max's summary of the situation as a bedridden mother, invalid brothers, "three bastard sons, a slutbitch of a wife," and a "lazy idle bugger" of a brother.

Teddy appears to have the same problem of definition. His picture of life in America with a marvelous wife, three sons, and a successful career is immediately qualified by Ruth. When the family leaves husband and wife together Teddy's attempts to get her away seem curiously unemotional and as far as she is concerned Venice, to which he has just taken her, has become only an echo of a previous speech by

Lenny. Her discussion with Lenny about the right shoes (right for what?)—so reminiscent of Davies in *The Caretaker*—leads her to reveal what, according to her, her former life was, to describe the attractions of modeling in country houses with bright lights. These lights, if necessary for photography, also suggest the glamour which she misses as housewife and mother, helping her husband to write his lectures.

Teddy is probably the most typical member of the family. He eats Lenny's cheese roll, for example, which leads into the discussion of Teddy as a member of the family. In America, Lenny suggests, Teddy has grown less outgoing and more sulky, more an individual than a member of the family:

But nevertheless we do make up a unit, Teddy, and you're an integral part of it. When we all sit round the backyard having a quiet gander at the night sky, there's always an empty chair standing in the circle which is in fact yours. And so when you at length return to us, we do expect a bit of grace, a bit of *je ne sais quoi*, a bit of generosity of mind, a bit of liberality of spirit, to reassure us. We do expect that. But do we get it? Have we got it? Is that what you've given us?[19]

Teddy makes no attempt to match this nonsense; his laconic reply is yes. In Pinter the art of being laconic is usually a strength—Lenny can defeat Max but Ruth can defeat Lenny precisely on this basis. But Teddy, who has been described as an Eichmann underneath, has rationalized his aggression to the point of being no longer human. Sam's revelation about Jessie can be ignored, but not Ruth's warning about becoming a stranger.

VIII   *The Morality*

I suppose we could, somewhere, nowadays, find a family like this, but the collection of actions and attitudes stretches credulity. To the average playgoer we have here material out of Zola or Dreiser treated like a comedy of manners (even to the famous contract scene, with Ruth as a modern Millamant!), where the wit and laughter contradict the shibboleths of the play. It is a technique that is quite different.

The characters represent the violent, bloody aspects of life: Max is a butcher, Joey a demolition man and spare-time boxer, and Lenny is a pimp. Jessie, the mother, was, apparently, promiscuous. The third son, however, is a philosopher who brings back his wife and the mother of his children to his family and watches unconcerned while they propose to turn her into a profit-making whore and, even more shockingly, while she barters her body as if it were a desirable corner site. Max's greeting in Act Two—"Where's the whore? Still in bed? She'll make us all animals"—evokes no response from anyone, including her husband. An obvious explanation would be Freudian. Thus States describes Teddy as an example of a "totally withdrawn libido" who is troubled by a hatred for women and homosexual tendencies, which is a family problem; Teddy therefore substitutes intellectual equilibrium for a proper sex life[20] while Esslin adds to this the dimension of old age, seeing the play as a combination of *Oedipus* and *King Lear*:

> The final image of *The Homecoming* therefore is the culmination of their Oedipal dreams: their mother, young and beautiful, has become available to them as a sexual partner, as a "whore," while the defeated father grovels on the floor pleading for some scraps of her sexual favours. This wish-fulfilment dream is the exact reversal of the real situation that faces a young son: the father in proud possession and the son rejected, oppressed, dominated.[21]

Certainly as the play entertains it touches hidden springs. If we compare *The Homecoming* with Joe Orton's *Loot*, Pinter's play seems more serious. Both plays deal with greed and violence, and neither play is interested in social reform or the correction of social abuses by laughter. Orton's play is a tale of intrigue and counterintrigue by totally amoral, greedy people which ultimately saves itself by never touching us where it might hurt. Pinter's play does hurt. Ruth's injunction not to become a stranger is important because it seems to be said with feeling whereas no other speech exhibits feeling. If we take Lenny's anecdotes recited to Ruth the point is not whether they are true or false but the matter-of-factness with which they are told. The characters are less concerned with having sex than with the idea of sexuality as it affects the others—and Teddy is totally unaffected. If Teddy modulates one set of concepts the "family" modulate their rather basic concepts of sex, profit, power. Our response ought not to be shock but simply astonishment. John Russell Brown has commented on the ambiguous nature of the title (but then most of Pinter's titles suggest the cozy):

> Teddy comes back home; and leaves for his other home; Ruth comes to a new home; Joey "comes" (in a sexual sense) for Ruth, in his own home; Sam seems, at the end, to come to his "last home." For all the characters truths come home.[22]

Some critics see the ending as a veritable household orgasm while others point out the irony that nobody comes (in fact "going the whole hog" may imply penetration and ejaculation can occur without that, particularly if Ruth is good at her job, which she obviously is!). What is important is the way Pinter handles these possibilities. He has, surely, learned from his film work how to suggest things as real and yet not real (or real only in the sense that they happen in the mind of the character—as illustrated by *Tea Party*). Worth has pointed out that in the scene in which Ruth rolls around with one brother, watched by her husband, Max is speaking all the time and what he says is commonplace: "It's as if a pornographic silent film has been dubbed with a sound sequence from a suburban family comedy."[23] This exactly describes what happens in the play. It is a modern, cinematic version of *The Way of the World*. And Teddy has withdrawn, become a stranger: he is too dead to have dreams or fantasies or even tell lies.

IX   *The Philosophy*

Stuart Hall, in his review of the play in *Encore* (July-August 1965), suggested that Teddy's long speech was important as the philosophical center of the play. But Lenny, too, has long speeches that are not simply anecdotes. The philosophical threads recall *The Dwarfs*. The family constantly harps on its pleasure at having a doctor in the house (though there is something funny in having a Ph.D. in philosophy), yet in the action of the play it is Lenny and Ruth who speculate. Teddy seems to be philosophical in the most restricted sense. It is Lenny who asks questions, who seeks the true facts of his existence, and who on his first meeting with Teddy and later Ruth speculates on the sameness and difference of things, and argues *like* a philosopher:

I mean there are lots of things which tick in the night, don't you find that? All sorts of objects, which, in the day, you couldn't call anything else but commonplace. They give you no trouble, but in the night any given one of a number of them is liable to start letting out a bit of a tick. Whereas you look at these objects in the day and they're just commonplace. They're quiet as mice during the daytime. So . . . all things being equal : . . this question of me saying it was the clock that woke me up, well, that could very easily prove something of a false hypothesis.[24]

Of course Ruth can undercut this with a glass of water. But again, in Act Two, it is Lenny who mockingly probes Teddy's philosophy which is shown as incredibly specialized. Granted that he can reject the "logical incoherence in the central affirmation of Christian theism" as outside his province, Lenny's later discussion on what merits reverence merits, surely, some answer? And the business of being and not being ought to fall into any philosopher's province? When Teddy philosophically pronounces that a table is, simply, a table he is refusing to play the game, which he loses because Lenny can then ironically appeal to Joey in admiration at this certainty. But Lenny loses when Ruth joins in. As Quigley observes:

> She cuts short the developing discussion on the ontology of tables and devastatingly demonstrates that from her point of view such issues (and, of course, Teddy's whole career) are monumentally irrelevant. Words, games, she suggests, are much less important than the fact that the mouth lives and the lips move. The physical world and, of course, her physical charms stand in need of physical, not mental exploration.[25]

But, of course, she is merely shifting the game into her own territory, not making any statement or reaching any conclusion. Similarly Esslin seems wrong when he says that she has resigned herself to being a passive object of desire: "Having failed in her marriage, Ruth is in a state of existential despair, a deep accidie, which is both fully understandable and completely motivates her behavior. She has tried to fight her own nature and she has been defeated by it. Now she yields to it, and surrenders beyond caring."[26] This hardly describes the woman who conducts the famous contract scene. If she is in existential despair then she can hardly have a nature to fight. Like Stella Ruth knows when to speak and when to keep silent. And like a good existentialist she continues to become her identity. She has tried wife and mother, daughter in law and sister in law, but none of these roles is final. The role of whore must not be regarded as final either. Teddy, on the other hand, is wedded to essences; he wants there to be no change. He even fails to notice that there have been changes—Lenny now has his room downstairs, for example—against which intellectual equilibrium is powerless.

X *Some Conclusions on* The Homecoming

When Ruth tells Teddy not to become a stranger she calls him Eddie—which is clearly a private name for him. The philosophy in the play is a psychological weapon rather than part of a debate. Teddy, according to Pinter, behaves at the end in character—what would have happened if he had interfered? He would have had a fight on his hands and this man would avoid that.[27] We must take Ruth's option as something to be tried as she had tried marriage with Teddy; and if it does not work. . . . Or, as Pinter put it:

If this has been a happy marriage it wouldn't have happened. But she didn't want to go back to America with her husband, so what the hell's she going to do? She's misinterpreted deliberately and used by this family. But eventually she comes back with a whip. She says "if you want to play this game I can play it as well as you." She does not become a harlot. At the end of the play she's in possession of a certain kind of freedom. She can do what she wants, and it is not at all certain she will go off to Greek Street. But even if she did, she would not be a harlot in her own mind.[28]

Yet another convention challenged, surely, is that the label "wife" in a failed marriage is little different from "whore."

Terms like "comedy" and "tragedy" do not seem to apply to a play like *The Homecoming*. In many ways it strikes a tragic note, even if we cannot pin down whose tragedy it is. But the play is a comedy if by comedy we mean adjustment to life, compromise with the status quo. The central theme could have been that of *The Lover* (a woman is both wife and whore), but the husband here disturbs that view because he will not even play the role of husband. It may be possession—though each character has his own room. There is little compassion or humanity in the play, though the rich sentiments of family affection and love flow like treacle through the play—contradicted, ironic, and phoney. Life being the black and greedy affair it is, one can act like Sam, who pretends to believe in goodness (and is probably dead at the end of the play), or like Ted, who refuses to get involved, turns his back on it, and becomes a stranger to life forever. Or one can fight, like Max and Joey. Or one can fight and win, like Ruth. Only Lenny remains at the end of the play uninvolved but not free, not lost, and certainly not overcome by Ruth's physical weapons. Apprehensive, certainly, but clearly the fun is not yet over.

CHAPTER 7

Off Stage

NOT entirely off stage, since this chapter will also look at Pinter as an actor; but mainly it is concerned with those activities which vied with play writing for Pinter's attention and, perhaps, distracted him from his work in the theater.

I *Pinter as Actor*

Pinter began as an actor. After playing Macbeth and Romeo at Hackney Downs Grammar School in 1947 and 1948 he appeared for the first time professionally in 1950 in "Focus on Football Pools," for the BBC Home Service, and in 1951 as Abergavenny in *Henry the Eighth,* for the BBC Third Program. From 1951–52 he toured in Shakespearean repertory with Anew McMaster's company (which he celebrates in *Mac,* 1968), and in 1953 he acted in Donald Wolfit's classical season at the King's Theatre, Hammersmith. Pinter spent the years 1954–57 acting in repertory in provincial theaters under the stage name of David Baron: "All the time acting was the only way I could conceive of earning any money. That was my life and work, and I did actually act consistently, more or less, for about ten years. I was writing all the time, but I never imagined that writing would gradually take over." In fact Pinter went to two drama schools, though neither was particularly useful to him: "I was very unhappy at the first one, which was R.A.D.A. I was much too young and I really hated it. Everyone seemed to be so sophisticated and know exactly where they were. I certainly didn't, and eventually I left. I faked a nervous breakdown and walked out and went to Lord's and watched Washbrook late-cutting. Later on I went to the Central School which was fine, but I only stayed there a year."[1] Since the writing took over he has continued to act, sometimes in his own plays: Goldberg at Cheltenham in 1960, Mick in *The Caretaker* at the Duchess Theatre in 1961, and Lenny in *The Homecoming* at Watford in 1969, as well as television
128

appearances as Seeley in *A Night Out* (1960) and Stott in *The Basement* (1967). He also appeared in *The Servant* and *Accident*. His most recent appearance, to date, was as an Irish drunk in his own dramatization, written in 1971, of Aidan Higgins's novel *Langrishe, Go Down* (1966)—a novel which won prizes and was favorably compared with the novels of Samuel Beckett. Pinter declined to direct but appeared in this story of three middle-aged Irish spinsters and a German philosophy student in a house in Ireland in the 1930s.

II *Pinter as Director*

Pinter directed his own play *The Birthday Party* in Oxford and Cambridge in 1958 and the same play for the Stephen Joseph Theater in Scarborough in 1959 (where the cast included David Campton as Petey and Alan Ayckbourn as Stanley); he directed *The Room* for the Hampstead Theatre Club in 1960 and *The Collection*, with Peter Hall, at the Aldwych in 1962. He directed *The Lover* and *The Dwarfs* (assisted by Guy Vaesen) at the Arts Theatre Club in London in 1963 and *The Birthday Party*, again, at the Aldwych in 1964, since when he seems to have preferred to leave his own plays to Peter Hall and direct plays by other writers: "I've come to think it's a mistake. I work much as I write, just moving from one thing to another to see what's going to happen next. One tries to get the thing . . . *true*. But I rarely get it. I think I'm more useful as the author closely involved with a play: as a director I think I tend to inhibit the actors, because however objective I am about the text and try not to insist that *this is what's meant*, I think there is an obligation on the actors too heavy to bear."[2]

Pinter's choice of plays by other writers, like his film work, reflects some kind of affinity with his own work. In 1967 he directed Robert Shaw's *The Man in the Glass Booth* and John Russell Taylor agreed that he was better here than when directing his own plays. In 1969 he directed *The Innocents* by William Archibald (out of Henry James) at the Morosco Theater, New York, and, in 1970, *Exiles* by James Joyce at the Mermaid Theatre, London, with Vivien Merchant in the cast. Subsequently this production went to the Aldwych in 1971. Esslin detected a deep sympathy with Joyce which made this production so clear and elegant: "What was it that drew Pinter to a play, which, outwardly at least is in the style and spirit of Ibsen? In fact, of course, Joyce was the most modern of modern writers, his work contains all the preoccupations of today's avant-garde. Behind the problem of marital morals in *Exiles,* there lie unplumbed depths of psychological insight . . . there is much here . . . of Ruth's nonchalance about sex in Pinter's own *The Homecoming.* On one level this is uncompromisingly honest Edwardian free thinking, on another it is sexual fantasy right out of Pinter's *The Lover.*"[3]

In 1973 Pinter became an associate director under Peter Hall at the National Theatre, and in October of that year it was announced that he would direct John Hopkins's *Always Another Time,* which opened in May 1974, as *Next of Kin.* In November 1975 it was announced that he would direct *The White Devil,* but in fact he directed *Blithe Spirit* in June 1976, a play clearly more in the spirit of his own work. Sandy Wilson, reviewing the production in *Plays and Players* (August 1976), wrote:

I thought I was pretty familiar with *Blithe Spirit,* but Mr. Pinter gave me a whole new angle on it: in his interpretation—and, considering his own plays, this should not come as a surprise—it is not so much about disembodied spirits cavorting around their former haunts as about human relationships, or, rather the failure of humans to relate to each other.

I'm not sure . . . what Coward intended, but it certainly shows a new facet of the play; the only trouble is that by concentrating on the marital infelicities of the Condomines it does rather leave the other principal, poor Madame Arcati, out in the cold.

Pinter's next production at the National Theatre was *Close of Play* (1979), the last, so far, of a close association with Simon Gray. He directed *Butley* (with Alan Bates) in 1971, *Otherwise Engaged* in London in 1975 and New York in 1977, and *The Rear Column* in 1978. It was with *Butley,* too, that he made his debut as a film director. *Butley* covers a day in which Butley loses everything, in which brilliant wit cannot conceal his emotional vulnerability nor shield him from the various messengers of doom who enter his untidy office. As David L. Hirst pointed out in the program note to the Curzon Cinema presentation: "in his control of emotion through a refinement of style Butley is in direct line from the rakes and wits of Restoration comedy, but unlike them, he is a loser."

III *Pinter's Work for the Cinema*

In an interview with John Russell Taylor in *Sight and Sound* (Autumn 1966) Pinter voiced his views on film and drama:

I do so hate the becauses of drama. Who are we to say that this happens because that happened, that one thing is the consequence of another? How do we know? What reason have we to suppose that life is so neat and tidy? The most we know for sure is that the things which have happened have happened in a certain order: any connection we think we see, or choose to make, are pure guesswork. Life is much more mysterious than plays make it out to be. And it is this mystery which fascinates me: what happens between the words, what happens when no words are spoken. . . . In this film [*Accident*] everything happens, nothing is explained. It has been pared down and down, all unnecessary words and actions are eliminated. If it is interesting to see a man cross a room, then we see him do it; if not, then we leave out the insignificant stages of the action. I think you'll be surprised at the directness, the simplicity with which Losey is directing this film: no elaborations, no odd angles, no darting about. Just a level, intense look at people, at things. As though if you look at them hard enough they will give up their secrets. Not that they will, for however much you see and guess at there is always that something more. . . .

The technique of leaving out insignificant stages was particularly useful to Pinter, and he soon incorporated it into his stage work. He has worked on three films, so far, with Losey, who had to leave Hollywood for Europe in 1953 because of the effects of McCarthyism, and Losey has recorded his pleasure at working with Pinter because "he is a poet." Of the script for *Accident* he remembers: "Although we talked about it many times and worked it out together, when he sat down to write it he gave it a poetic and lyrical rhythm which was an enormous help to me."[4]

So far Pinter has written scripts for eight films, six of which have been published and six of which have been filmed. *Five Screenplays* (1971) contains *The Servant* (1963), *The Pumpkin Eater* (1964), *The Quiller Memorandum* (1966), *Accident* (1967), and *The Go-Between* (1971). It would be helpful to know what form these screenplays take. Do they represent final drafts before production or postproduction scripts? The screenplay of *Proust* represents the final stage before filming (which has not taken place). Pinter also wrote the screenplay for *The Last Tycoon* and in 1979 it was announced that Karel Reisz would produce and direct *The French Lieutenant's Woman* from a screenplay by Pinter based on the novel by John Fowles.

Obviously Pinter is part of a team; he acts as go-between for text and screenplay. But it is also true to say that his screenplays contain not merely dialogue which is Pinteresque but also mirror some of his basic themes and obsessions. In a field where the director is the superstar the fact that Pinter has made a mark as a writer is a tribute to his talent. The film, too, presumably provided him with some sort of financial security to permit him to write as he pleased.

IV *Pinter's Plays as Films*

Pinter's first play to be filmed was *The Caretaker* (discussed in Chapter 4); subsequently two other plays, *The Birthday Party* and *The Homecoming*, have been made into films. There is general agreement that the film of *The Birthday Party* is a faithful transfer of the play to the screen, which, though directed by William Friedkin, remained definitely the creation of its author. It was, according to Penelope Mortimer (the *Observer*, February 15, 1970), "a photographed play in three acts," though there were a few ventures at moves out of doors (less so than in *The Caretaker*): the Rolls carrying the visitors glides through the streets to a sound like wheels on gravel and there were shots of the desolate sea-front and empty deck chairs. *The Homecoming*, too, presented the play as film. Pinter's most successful work has been the translation of other people's work to the screen.

V The Servant

Maugham's story attracted Pinter because, as he explained in connection with "The Examination," he saw it as a battle for domination. When asked about the changes Pinter replied:

Well I don't know exactly. I followed it up, I think I did change it in a number of ways. I cut out the particular a narrator in fact which I didn't think was very valuable to a film but I think I did change it quite a lot one way or another but I kept to the main core at the same time the end is not quite the same ending that it was in the book. I must have *carte blanche* you know to explore it.[5]

The elimination of the narrator, Richard Merton, is certainly the most important change since his relationship with Tony is the oddest thing in the novel. But Pinter has also made Tony's background more vague. He left Cambridge where he was reading law to join the army in 1939 and since his parents were dead and he was unmarried the army became his home and family. At the beginning of the novel he has returned from the Orient to study law again. He introduces Merton to his girl friend, Sally Grant, and moves into a furnished apartment with a new servant, Barrett, whom Merton finds repellent. But Barrett is perfect for Tony because he "insulates me from a cold drab world." Although Sally is in love with Tony they have never been lovers and she worries about Barrett's influence but Merton assures her that Tony is perfectly normal in his sexual habits. Merton, too, becomes worried, however. Tony refuses to get rid of Barrett even if keeping him means taking on his niece as a maid. This niece, Vera, a girl of about sixteen, soon gets Tony into bed with her. When Vera goes back to Manchester for a holiday Tony goes to Cornwall. Merton, passing the house, sees a light burning and, thinking Tony has returned unexpectedly, lets himself in to find Barrett and Vera together in Tony's bed. When Tony learns of this Barrett reveals that Vera is his fiancée and points out that servant and master are more or less in the same position. Tony throws them both out and goes to stay with Merton; and, after a night out with a nameless woman, returns to Cornwall. When he returns from Cornwall fresh and healthy he resumes his old life with Sally until he meets Barrett in a pub and takes him back. Sally marries another man and leaves for Rhodesia while Tony settles down to the comforts that Barrett alone can provide. Merton recognizes defeat, for Barrett has replaced the only woman who loved Tony—his nanny. When Merton meets Vera, now a prostitute, he learns that Barrett knew about everything all the time but when he rushes off to tell Tony Tony is uninterested. The arrival of a very young girl to amuse Tony and Barrett ends the novel.

The two problems of the film were the latent homosexuality that carried over from the novel in spite of the removal of the narrator, and the heroine. Susan's background in the film was vague—mainly because it was difficult to find the right actor to play the upperclass. Wendy Craig played it in her own basically Northern accent and Losey failed to justify the relationship. With the elimination of the narrator the role of Susan became more important (she is a very minor character in the novel); in the film it is Susan and Tony who discover Barrett and Vera in bed together (just when they themselves are going to get into it); and it is Susan who goes to Tony at the end to plead with him and is defeated by Barrett. There is also a certain symbolic significance in changing Tony from a lawyer to an architect whose father has just died leaving him vaguely rich and free—to do whatever he likes. He has dreams of building great cities in Brazil but produces only a stunted obelisk and is gradually reduced to doing crossword puzzles (a hint from the novel that Pinter intensifies).

Pinter also adds the games his characters play—a ball game on the stairs, and a sinister game of hide-and-seek in the shower (apparently a private joke about the film *Psycho*) which suggest the gradual degradation of Tony. At the end there is a party, not just one girl, which Losey intended to balance the homosexual nuances: "I also wanted to make it very clear at the end that this was a kind of *ménage à trois*, that there were all sorts of crossing of sex and not just homosexual implications; and that it was a story of the destruction not only of the master but of the servant."[6] The screenplay gave greater ambiguity to Barrett, who in the Maugham novel is simply wicked. For Pinter Barrett needs his master and is hopelessly adrift outside the master's rooms. So Losey saw the film as about servility "both of the servants and the masters. It is a product of the general corruption amidst which we live, the kind of hypocrisy common to all of us."[7] Both Losey and Pinter regarded the servant as a victim and sympathetic, though Bogarde's portrayal of that role (like Pleasance's portrayal of Davies in the film of *The Caretaker*) made sympathy difficult. Losey feels that a remark of his—that it was the story of a Faust—obscured the intended interpretation, which was to work on two levels—sociological and sexual— and that the homosexuality was only latent. But the games played are far from innocent and the memories of army days are not quite balanced by one orgy with very young girls; whatever the interpretation this Faust sells his soul for a soufflé.

Pinter adds a few revue-type sketches—in a restaurant, at the Mountsets, and in Nick's diner. Many critics liked the wit of the film and some, like Penelope Gilliatt (*Observer*, November 17, 1963), noted that the room had now widened into a malignant house, an idea fruitfully explored by Taylor:

Tony's house is a sophisticated upper-class extension of the recurrent symbol in Pinter's early plays, the room-womb which offers a measure of security in an insecure world, an area of light in the surrounding darkness. But here the security is a trap sprung on the occupant by his own promptings and by the servant who embodies them and knows too well how to exploit them.[8]

VI   The Pumpkin Eater

Directed by Jack Clayton (whose *Room at the Top*, 1958, pioneered a movement in British films), this film was based on the novel by Penelope Mortimer written in 1962. The title is taken, appropriately, from a nursery rhyme about Peter, who had a wife and could not keep her, so he put her in a pumpkin shell and there he kept her very well.

The novel tells, from the wife's point of view and intimately, the story of a clash between herself and her husband—the husband escaping from his wife and children through work and affairs with other women and the wife, who just wants to go on having children. There seems to be, also, the usual modern implication that success spoils life. The heroine, at the beginning of the novel, is having some sort of breakdown— she has had several husbands and a lot of children. She traps her husband into giving her another child, but is then herself trapped into having a hysterectomy. At this point she discovers that her husband— a script-writer for films!—is having affairs:

> "Nothing matters now, I suppose. And yet something does."
> "Of course something does. The future."
> "No. Not the future. The truth."
> "Can't you see? Before you knew the truth, we were happy. What's the good in ferreting out the truth all the time? It's always unpleasant."
> "Is it only lies that are pleasant?"
> "Usually. That's why people tell them. To make life bearable."[9]

By the end of the novel she is reconciled with her husband and they are all together in a large tower (symbolic?) on a hill in the country. As she herself says in the final paragraph:

I have tried to be honest with you, although I suppose that you really have been more interested in my not being honest. Some of these things happened, and some were dreams. They are all true, as I understood truth. They are all real, as I understood reality.

This is a clue to Pinter's interest, but, for myself, the lady remained uninteresting in both the film and the novel. *The Sunday Times* (Color Supplement, April 26, 1964) felt that the film had been remarkably faithful to the novel and that the dialogue showed Pinter's "mastery of the casually overheard remark, significant in its sinister ambiguity" and admirably suited to the depiction of a "nervous breakdown against a background of meaningless social activity." The main impression of the film, however, was visual rather than verbal and David Robinson, in the *Financial Times*, argued that there was a tension between the objectivity of the camera and the subjectivity of the actress playing the role. In the *Observer* (July 19, 1964) Penelope Gilliatt felt that we do not know enough about the central character to prevent the film from seeming a shade mechanical while Dilys Powell, in *The Sunday*

Times, praised the film for its elegance but saw the film as Clayton's not Pinter's.

VII   The Quiller Memorandum

If *The Pumpkin Eater* was well received but no more, this film was even less successful, though to my mind it was more interesting and significant. *The Quiller Memorandum* (1966) was an adaptation of *The Berlin Memorandum* by Adam Hall (Elleston Trevor), directed by Michael Anderson (who had been the original director for *The Servant*) and filmed by Ivan Foxwell. In spite of a distinguished cast including Sir Alec Guinness, Max von Sydow, George Sanders, Senta Berger, and George Segal as Quiller it was generally regarded as nothing more than an average spy thriller. Scenes such as the fourth sequence, where George Sanders and Robert Flemyng have lunch in a London club, are clearly written by Pinter, but, of course, the whole story is set in Pinterland: lies (that is, cover stories), sex, violence, and betrayal suit him perfectly and at the end the partial failure of Quiller to get rid of the neo-Nazi movement (Inge remains, surrounded by eager and obedient children, ready to do the work she must do and wants to do) puts Quiller, for all his James Bond glamour, firmly in a Pinter setting, where is is cheated of success and the girl.

VIII   Accident

Critics were unanimous in their praise for *Accident,* however, when it appeared in February 1967. *Accident,* an adaptation of Nicholas Mosley's stream-of-consciousness novel, directed by Joseph Losey, was described by Penelope Houston, in the *Spectator* (February 17, 1967), as a "compellingly articulate movie" and both Penelope Gilliatt, in the *Observer,* and Dilys Powell, in *The Sunday Times,* agreed. Both the author and the scriptwriter appeared in the film in minor roles and Bogarde and Merchant played the central couple, a philosopher, forty years old, nine years married, with a pregnant wife, thinking back to explain the accident which saved his marriage, and the motives of himself and the other two men involved with the young Austrian student Anna. Stephen sums up the experiences of the novel with the comment: Remember it happy; the sun in your eyes. But Pinter ends the film with another accident as the family dog runs across the road. Bogarde described the film as "a perfectly hand-crafted piece of work from the first shot to the last"[10] while Losey saw it as "a question of relationships of men to women and women to men, and men to men as against men to women, which is something I am deeply concerned with."[11] A philosopher whose home life is shattered by an intruding girl recalls *The Homecoming* and Anna, like Ruth, fulfills various needs: mistress, whore, earth mother, and possibly wife to the student William. But Stephen is no Teddy. He is intelligent, enquiring, and he is married to a sensitive and understanding wife. Even so, in the film he enjoys Anna before he gives her up—and he does so on terms that suggest blackmail since he conceals the fact that she was driving or even in the car. Pinter has wisely cut out the philosophical arguments of Mosley (Wittgenstein versus existentialism, empiricism versus metaphysics), and he has also removed references by Stephen to himself as a Jew (particularly relevant considering Anna's Austrian background and the visit to a stately home). Where a first-person narrative brings the reader close to Stephen, Pinter and the camera eye render the narrative objectively. The accident is the result of a collision among four people, and we can take no sides, only perhaps see that nothing ever is accidental. Who exploits whom—is a question that cannot be answered: "Is Anna, who has excited the passions of three men and played them off against one another, the exploiter? Are the men, who have fought over her like cunning animals, disregarding the needs of their wives, the exploiters? Is William, who has played so hard and so brutally, really the object of our sympathy? We leave the cinema caught in the Pinter web of verification or the lack of it."[12] The games from *The Servant* appear here as a cricket match and the public school ritual at Lord Codrington's described by Stephen, correctly, as "a murderous game"—both looking forward, with all the associations of class and sex, to the cricket match in *The Go-Between*.

IX   The Go-Between

This was an adaptation of the novel of the same name by L. P. Hartley, published in 1953. It concerns the traumatic initiation into sex during one long hot August in 1900 of Leo Colston recollected by the still unmarried Colston in the present—"all dried-up inside," as the novel puts it. It portrays sexual heat, class differences, the baffling nature of adult language to the literal mind of a young boy, and begins with the opening lines of the novel: "The past is a foreign country. They do things differently there." The attractiveness of the film lies mainly in the leisurely evocation of Edwardian life in the Norfolk countryside, the sort of elegant life remembered in *No Man's Land*; but unless one knows the story the initiation in the film is not made clear enough to justify its crippling effect on the hero. But the past haunting the present, and imagined as happening in the present—which film can do— connects with the plays of this period being worked at by Pinter.

X   The Last Tycoon

Work began on *The Last Tycoon* in 1975 and the director was, finally, Elia Kazan. The film is based on Scott Fitzgerald's unfinished novel of that name (1941), and though a dream factory is a good situation for Pinter the choice of so English a writer seemed curious. Gordon Gow, in *Films and Filming* (March 1977), described the adaptation as spare and sensitive and respectful—using a great deal exactly as Fitzgerald set it down and not using the notes on the ending left by Fitzgerald so that the film is "curtailed, only slightly rounded off," thus throwing the emphasis on Stahr's efforts to recreate his former love life rather than on the social background; it is Stahr's dreamworld rather than Hollywood that occupies the film.

XI   Remembrance of Things Past

Early in 1972 Losey was asked if he would like to work on a film version of *A La Recherche du Temps Perdu*. Pinter was offered the screenplay and suggested Barbara Bray as adviser. The revised version of 1973, *The Proust Screenplay*, was published in 1978—the film has, unfortunately, not been made yet. Pinter recalls that it was "the best working year of my life" and, to my mind, it shows.

It also shows that we should not regard these activities as a distraction from the theater but an enrichment of Pinter's talents, as seen in the plays he continued to write. Herold Hobson, in *The Sunday Times* (June 1965), complained that *The Homecoming* was Pinter's cleverest play, but he was troubled by "the complete absence from the play of any moral comment whatsoever. To make such a comment does not necessitate an author's being conventional or religious; it does necessitate, however, his having made up his mind about life, his having come to some decision. . . . We have no idea what Mr. Pinter thinks of Ruth or Teddy or what value their existence has. They have no relation to life outside themselves. They live; their universe lives: but not the universe." This seems a curious judgment to make on Pinter. He has always, in a way, played at being objective camera. Here he is being accused of the same emotional coldness that is charged against Alain Resnais—much of whose wit and humor is lost in translation—but like Pinter Resnais was seeking a new form, a new syntax. Consider this description of *L'Année dernière a Marienbad:*

The image of Marienbad: ornate, baroque, stylized, is interesting for itself as pure setting. Moreover, there is a plot, contrary to popular belief. The relationship between X and M, for example, if examined in isolation, is no different from what we might expect in an ambitious Hollywood film. They play a macho game that is nevertheless civilized (in the sense of utilizing upper class manners). The struggle for A's affections takes place here and now and the main metaphor for it is the match game which M and X engage in several times during the course of the film. In addition, the M-X-A relationships are set in the context of a large group of other guests, none of whom has to deal with the persuasions of the main narrative. They are hazily outlined, but they know a battle is going on between X and M (and X and A). . . . [13]

Love and memory are transient, and as Pinter grows older this must press in on him more acutely; the room can be invaded, and the inhabitants grow old—"through his art, the Hackney Jew—like the French half-Jew, Marcel Proust—attempts to capture the moment and set it above the uncertainties that time brings."[14]

CHAPTER 8

Remembrance of Things Past

I N *Leviathan* Hobbes defines imagination as decaying sense and
points out that when we want to signify that the sense is old and
fading we call it memory: "So that *Imagination* and *Memory* are but
one thing, which for divers considerations hath divers names." Characters in Pinter have always told stories about their pasts which
"explain" their present state; the truth or untruth of these stories is less
important than the effect they have on the antagonist. More and more
Pinter has explored his themes of love, loneliness, failure, and power
in terms of the past—and our unwillingness to remember it except as
it suits the present struggle.

I "*Night*"

The Times (January 10, 1968) announced a new play by Pinter, the
first since *The Homecoming*, which would be produced by the RSC
later that year or early in 1969; it was "about a man and a woman and
what they say." But by January 21 the Lord Chamberlain had
informed Pinter that the play would be banned unless certain phrases
were deleted. Pinter refused and the play was not performed until censorship ended on September 27, 1968. *Landscape* was then performed
in a double bill with *Silence* at the Aldwych in 1969 and in New York
in 1970. Also in 1969 a short sketch by Pinter called "Night" was
included in *Mixed Doubles*—"an entertainment on marriage"—originally presented at the Hampstead Theatre Club in February 1969 and
transferred in its final form in April to the Comedy Theatre. It consisted of eight short plays, each for two characters, by dramatists like
Ayckbourn, Bowen, Campton, and James Saunders, linked by monologues written by George Melly and covering the progress of married
life from the honeymoon to the grave. "Night" is a brief discussion
between a woman and a man "in their forties" who may be married
(they certainly have children) about the first time they met and made
140

love—a meeting that affected their lives considerably. But their memories of that first night are contradictory: Did they meet at a party or on a bridge? Did he make love on a rubbish dump or pressed against some railings? Perhaps he remembers an incident with another girl? Perhaps she recalls an incident with another man . . . ? Robert Cushman (*Plays and Players*, June 1969) writes of the "glassy elegance" of the piece but, in fact, the tone is quiet and elegiac, in tune with both *Landscape* and *Silence*.

II   Landscape

Landscape was published in a limited edition in 1968 and together with *Silence* (and "Night") in 1969. The words that could not be spoken on the English stage could be broadcast on the English radio, and so the first performance of *Landscape* took place on April 25 on the BBC Third Program and was repeated on May 21 the same year. The parts of Beth and Duff were played by Peggy Ashcroft and Eric Porter. It seemed so essentially a play for radio, consisting as it does of two monologues, that we must remember that it was written as a stage play. As the two monologues proceed we watch Beth and Duff transform their ordinary world into something lyrical—and we are struck by the importance of the visual. The play is full of physical references and images:

None of his plays introduces more reference to persons off-stage who are of importance to what is told of the characters; none is so descriptive of objects and movements whether of people, dogs, ducks, children or machines; none has more references to the sea, rain, shadow or sunlight. The activity portrayed through the two enigmatical presences and their voices is highly contrasted. . . . [1]

That they are monologues is to a certain extent indicated by the stage directions:

DUFF refers normally to BETH, but does not appear to hear her voice.
BETH never looks at DUFF, and does not appear to hear his voice.

The original instruction for Beth read:

BETH, in her speech, never refers to DUFF and does not appear to hear his voice.

But Pinter also insists in the same directions that both characters are relaxed, in no sense rigid.

Beth opens the play with the memory of a day on the beach with her lover, observed by two women. Her thoughts are of the past, never of the present; when Duff intervenes he speaks mainly of what he has been doing in the last day or two. If Beth's thoughts wander away from the beach—a hotel bar, or being picked up by his car at the cross-roads—they continue in the same vein: her relationship with this man from whom she wanted a child, who was gentle to her, who kissed her softly and was her true love. Duff, on the other hand, provides us with information about why they are there, in the kitchen of a country house which has been left to them by a Mr. Sykes for whom they had worked as housekeeper/cook and chauffeur/handyman. Did he leave them the house because they were good servants or was there a closer relationship between him and Beth? When did the relationship between Beth and Duff cease? According to Duff it was when he saw her banging the gong as she had always done when Mr. Sykes was alive which drove him so wild that he tore off her scissors, chain of keys, and thimble and tried to rape her in the hall. Or is this, too, fantasy? The basic difference in the two stories is between a remembered, idyllic past and a brutal present. We may assume that Beth loved Mr. Sykes, who betrayed her by bringing in other women and who is now dead; or Beth has been confronted with a confession of Duff's infidelity and then retreats into the memory of the good times they had before he became unfaithful; or, faced with that unfaithfulness, Beth retaliates with the fantasy of having had a lover. A letter from Pinter to the director of the first German performance in 1970 which was published in the program (against Pinter's intentions) observed:

The man on the beach is Duff. I think there are elements of Mr. Sykes in her memory of this Duff which she might be attributing to Duff, but the man remains Duff. I think that Duff detests and is jealous of Mr. Sykes, although I do not believe that Mr. Sykes and Beth were ever lovers.

I formed these conclusions after I had written the plays and after learning about them through rehearsals.[2]

Of course they may simply be director's notes, aids to performance, which explains why Pinter was angry at having them published as a statement about the meaning of the play. The alternatives in the monologues are power and energy in the present (though the energy is associated with coarseness, particularly in sex) and an impulse to retreat from life into a remembered past where everything is tender, beautiful, undisturbed. The past is a foreign country where they do things differently. Some critics responded to the play as a celebration of life, while others saw it as ending in despair. By comparison with *Silence* it is certainly cheerful.

III   Silence

In *Landscape* the gangsters from the past are memories. Beth longs for gentleness but Mr. Sykes, her gentle employer, betrays her and flaunts women before her, becoming a Duff. Her loneliness, however, is more companionable than that of Ellen, the heroine of *Silence*, who has failed to make a choice at all. *Silence* is another country play, but there are three characters, Ellen and two men, Rumsey (a man of forty) and Bates (a man in his middle thirties), located only on three stools in three lighted areas. Rumsey and Bates were two medium quick bowlers who opened for Hampshire and Sussex, respectively, but Pinter has denied that he thought of them consciously when writing *Silence*—he just looked in his mind for two country names. The idea may have occurred consciously, however, when he came to write *No Man's Land*. The three characters, each in his/her own room, tell the story which, as Esslin points out, breaks chronology more decisively than flashbacks. The story, then, is presented from three points of view and from two or three points in time, unfolding a simple tale summarized by Esslin as follows: Ellen grows up in the country and two men fall in love with her. Rumsey breaks off with her, advising her to look for younger men. She may have gone off with Bates but she loved Rumsey so that relationship also broke up. So Rumsey stays on his farm contented but lonely while Bates and Ellen stay in the town, isolated and longing for the country. Robert Cushman, in *Plays and Players* (August 1969), found the experience rather like listening to fragments of an unwritten Hardy novel and pointed out that if the comparison was to be with Beckett at least Beckett had solved the practical problem of presenting his characters by putting them into urns. A better analogy might be with *Huis Clos* by Sartre, in which Pinter had acted shortly before; this play might be his version of death.

IV   Old Times

In *The Times* (April 11, 1969) Pinter confessed that his plays were getting shorter: "...Words are so tender. One act plays are all I seem to be able to write at the moment. I doubt if I will ever write something mammoth." And in his acceptance speech at Hamburg, 1970, he confessed he found it ironic to be awarded something as a writer when "at the moment I am writing nothing and can write nothing. I don't know why. It's a very bad feeling. I know that, but I must say I want more than anything else to fill up a blank page again, and to feel that strange thing happen, birth through fingertips. When you can't write you feel you've been banished from yourself."

Old Times (1971) was certainly not a mammoth play; though it pretends to be in two acts the running time is about one and one-half hours, including an interval. The first draft came spontaneously, taking only three days to write—indeed it was, apparently, composed so quickly that the characters had no names and were simply designated A, B, and C in a piece called "Others with Dancers." The play was dedicated to Peter Hall, who directed it at the Aldwych, with Dorothy Tutin, Vivien Merchant, and Colin Blakely in the roles of Kate, Anna, and Deeley.

The lights go up at the beginning of the play on two of the three characters. Deeley and his wife, Kate, are talking about Anna, who stands in the dim light at the back of the stage. The memories are of twenty years ago, when their paths first crossed. Kate remembers Anna's fondness for stealing her knickers. Anna enters the lighted area and revives memories of the lively cultural life she and Kate enjoyed which Deeley counters with the recollection of how he first met Kate in an empty cinema showing the film *Odd Man Out*. The recollections that follow are all strategic, and consequently never quite match. Anna remembers Kate bringing a sobbing man back to their room who looked down at her as she lay on the bed; Deeley remembers looking at Anna's knickers (which would be Kate's?) at a party; and Anna remembers going with Kate to see *Odd Man Out*. Deeley recognizes the threat that their shared experiences will exclude him.

In Act Two Deeley and Anna talk about their first meeting and his meeting with Kate at the film *Odd Man Out* while Anna remembers a man looking at her knickers at a party (Kate had loaned them to her). Deeley tells Kate of his first meeting with Anna but then Kate remembers Anna dead on her bed. She also remembers bringing a man back to her room. Anna withdraws to her divan, Kate to hers and Deeley at first moves to Kate and lies in her lap. Then he gets up and moves to the armchair. There is silence and then the brightest of lighting as the play ends.

Out of such fragments we could make up a story but we must remember a comment by Anna in Act One: "There are some things one remembers even though they may never have happened. There are things I remember which may never have happened but as I recall them so they take place."

All we know "for certain" is that Deeley is probably some sort of artist who lives in a converted farmhouse with his wife, Kate; that Anna shared a room with Kate some twenty years ago and now, richly married, has flown over from Sicily for a visit. A. B. Young, in the *Financial Times*, found the play fascinating: "We are in a dream world, a world in which events have the appearance of logic but can't be connected together in logical sequence; and, as in dreams, we are quite incapable of detaching ourselves from what is being played out in front of us." However, where *Landscape* and *Silence* were also dream worlds, they were meditative; but here clearly we must respond more positively—a dissertation on the ambiguity of memory will not do—a battle is going on—for the room and the girl; and it is going on in terms of the one who can produce the best memory. Trussler's dislike of Pinter misleads him, as usual, here when he insists that the tricks played by the dramatist aren't experienced by the characters so that ambiguity has degenerated into "the merely mechanical and arbitrary." The play brings back old times but in new techniques—derived from film work and the experience of creating the verbal plays, *Landscape* and *Silence*. But here the medium is more accessible, indeed more commercially viable; but no less haunting. An intruder disturbs the room and a relationship posing the question whether husband or girl friend, present lover or past soul-mate, can best know the wife. The debate works in terms of producing a strong memory. It may be, of course, as Esslin suggests, that the whole play is a nightmare of Deeley's since he is the only character involved in the whole play, which would rather suggest that Anna and Kate might be aspects of the same woman. Deeley's hunted quality is reinforced, as is his Irishness, by the reference to the film *Odd Man Out* (1947), where James Mason played a hunted IRA gunman—gathering up echoes from McCann's hatred of betrayal in *The Birthday Party*. This is one solution to the question: is Anna there at the beginning in the flesh, or a ghost, or is the leap into her opening lines to be taken as a filmic effect avoiding the formalities of a conventional entrance: or, all three?

But these interpretations, if valid, blur the central debate over Kate, who seems to have little interest in memory or analysis, who remains silent, passive—though, as Taylor has pointed out, Pinter's women seem to get what they want in the end:

Men who act will always dominate men who stop to think; women think and act simultaneously, as though with some deep unquestioning instinct, and therefore dominate both. And perhaps, too, it helps that, like cats, they have no remembered loyalties, no encumbering ties with the past. Memory—which is just the problem of verification seen from another angle—is likely to be a liability, committing one always to live out and relive the past instead of living in and taking full advantage of the present.[3]

Kate is not merely the bone of contention, she is the strongest of the three: she accepts Deeley but only as a child—in her lap. And when she joins in and tells stories, like the other two characters, they are killing tales. She tells of dreaming of seeing them dead—an account which freezes the play in a way that anticipates the "ending" of *No Man's Land*—these characters seem forever in a kind of no man's land. The echoes here might be, as Katharine J. Worth suggests, from *Blithe Spirit:* "where a man calls up the ghost of his dead wife and finds himself between the living and the dead—until the first wife kills off the second and he has two ghosts on his hands. Elvira does suggest that Charles might have brought her back to discuss the old times; and here, too, it is a song that helps the seance along: 'Always.'"

There are echoes, too, of *Exiles*, which Pinter has also directed—the silent woman, probing husband, fear and nostalgia for the past, and even a faint glimmer of lesbianism in both plays; there is a kind of thread stretching from *Exiles* through *The Family Reunion* to *The Homecoming* and *Old Times.*[4] It is a quiet, short, elegiac, haunting play with disturbing undercurrents; ironically it hit the headlines when those hinted undercurrents came to the fore in Visconti's version of it, *Tanto Tempo Fa* (1973), which featured, prominently, masturbation and lesbianism![5]

V Monologue

Monologue, produced by BBC Television in 1973, was the only link between *Old Times* and *No Man's Land*. It is a simple memory play staged with a man addressing an empty chair, reminiscing about the past. That past, apparently, contained a friend and a black girl. Both friends were rivals for the girl and the friend seems to have won. The two friends were great games players and discussed literature and art, but the friend seems to have lapsed into mediocrity, though he may have had children by the black girl, whereas the narrator is success-ful—but, of course, alone: addressing only an empty chair. In, one might say, his own kind of *No Man's Land.*

VI   No Man's Land

No Man's Land, directed by Peter Hall, was first presented by the National Theatre (at the Old Vic) on April 23, 1975. The setting is a large room in northwest London, well but sparely furnished, whose central feature is an antique cabinet full of drinks. To this room the owner, Hirst, apparently a successful writer in his sixties, has brought a shabby-looking man, Spooner, also in his sixties, and is offering him a drink. Hirst has, we are told, picked up Spooner at a pub on Hamp-stead Heath. Hirst is drunk and it makes him morose and silent and Spooner, who claims he is a poet, rattles on to cover up this silence (after all he is getting free drinks and an audience) about himself, his inner strength which he claims comes from his detachment from human emotion. Spooner, clearly, is lonely and loveless and makes a virtue of the condition: he is a "free man." Hirst replies that it is a long time since we had a free man in this house—suggesting that there are others in the house and that he does not feel himself a free man. As Spooner goes on about his gracious past—keeping open house in the country for young poets, his wife pouring glasses of squash on summer evenings, Hirst replies that he, too, has done the same. Spooner grasps at a connection—"a memory of bucolic life"—which Hirst continues to explore:

HIRST: In the village church, the beams are hung with garlands, in honor
         of young women of the parish, reputed to have died virgin.
         Pause
         However the garlands are not bestowed on maidens only, but on
         all who die unmarried, wearing the white flower of a blameless life.

But Hirst soon withdraws from this image of blameless life and Spooner is compelled to improvise, unaided, until he proposes himself as a friend, an offer which Hirst declines:

HIRST: No.
        Pause
        No man's land . . . does not move . . . or change . . . or grow old
        . . . remains . . . forever.

Having said this Hirst falls to the floor and crawls out of the room on
all fours. Even this cannot shake Spooner's detachment; he has, he
claims, known all this before. Yet that detachment is shaken by the
entry of a younger man, Foster, who registers no surprise at finding a
stranger drinking in the room and calmly introduces him to the next
arrival, Briggs, as Mr. Friend. Where Foster is young, lively, and
almost effeminate, Briggs is older (in his forties), stocky, coarser, and
blunt. And Briggs recognizes the poet Spooner as a man who collects
dirty beer mugs from the tables at the Bulls Head in Chalk Farm.
Spooner fights back, however, and, when Foster talks about traveling,
insists that he, too, has traveled. He has been to Amsterdam, where he
might have painted a picture which would have had the puzzling title
The Whistler. But neither Briggs nor Foster is bothered by this puzzle
so Spooner goes on to invite them to his house in the country, where
they will be given the warmest of welcomes from his wife and two
daughters. Foster meets this challenge with an anecdote about the mysterious East, where a tramp who had rejected the coin thrown to him
made it disappear. As Spooner says, not a mystery but a con trick.
    Hirst now appears, loquacious, talking about a dream in which
someone was drowning and his photograph album which records his
remarkable past. He also asks to be introduced to Spooner. When
Spooner claims that it was he who was drowning Hirst collapses. They
all move to help him but Spooner claims the privilege of age:

He has grandchildren. As have I. As I have. We both have fathered. We are
of an age. I know his wants. Let me take his arm. Respect our age.

    But Briggs and Foster point out that they are there to protect Hirst
"against men of craft, against men of evil," a task they perform out of
love:

Listen, my friend. This man in this chair, he's a creative man. He's an artist.
We make life possible for him. We're in a position of trust. Don't try to drive
a wedge into a happy household. You understand me? Don't try to make a
nonsense out of family life.

Hirst recovers and asks for sandwiches and Briggs goes off to make them while Foster laments how he has to run the house and misses all those Siamese and Balinese girls. Briggs returns to point out that there is no bread, that the housekeeper is not doing his job, and, attacking Foster as a "neurotic poof," he leads Hirst firmly out of the room. Foster tells Spooner a story about meeting a man in the Australian desert who was carrying two umbrellas and asks him if he knows what it is like to be in a room when all the lights go out. He then switches off the lights, leaving Spooner in total darkness.

Act Two takes place the following morning. Spooner is still locked in the room but he claims that this, too, has happened to him before. When Briggs enters to offer him a champagne breakfast he says that he never touches food, though when he learns that it will be wasted (it was prepared for the financial adviser who has canceled his visit) he accepts because he abhors waste. However, he is careful to ask if the champagne is cold and insists that he is a champagne drinker; he knows his wines. Briggs, meanwhile explains how he first met Foster, who was asking the way to Bolsover Street (part of a one-way traffic system so complicated that once you get in you can never get out). But, as Briggs points out, Foster's version will be different. Spooner goes on at some length about his work as a poet, his newly formed poetry magazine, and the patronage of Lord Lancer, but Briggs tests this by pointing out that Foster is a poet in need of patronage since their boss, Hirst, won't help him.

Hirst now enters, calling Spooner Charles (and Briggs, Denson) and recalling their time together at Oxford, cricket in 1939, girl friends and the war, and claiming that he had an affair with Spooner's wife, Emily. Spooner retaliates by claiming that he deceived Hirst several times and was outraged by Hirst's "insane and corrosive sexual absolutism" which had not been restricted to women. He also attacks Hirst's literary abilities, particularly his failure to master the *terza rima*. Hirst is now outraged. This is not the Charles Weatherby he knew and he shifts into reminiscences about his photograph album where those who you thought were dead are still alive:

. . . from whom you will receive a sidelong glance, if you can face the good ghost. Allow the love of the good ghost. They possess all that emotion . . . trapped. Bow to it. It will assuredly never release them, but who knows . . . what relief . . . it may give to them . . . who knows how it may quicken . . . in their chains, in their glass jars. You think it cruel . . . to quicken them, when they are fixed, imprisoned? No. Deeply, deeply, they wish to respond to your touch, to your look, and when you smile, their joy . . . is unbounded. And so I say to you, tender the dead, as you would yourself be tendered, now, in what you describe as your life.

Briggs replies brutally, that they are all blank: the blank dead. And he refuses to pass the bottle when Hirst orders him to or to be dismissed from his post. Foster now enters to announce that it is time for Hirst to take his morning walk which Hirst refuses to do since he has work to do: "I can't possibly. I have too many things to do, I have an essay to write. A critical essay. We'll have to check the files, find out what it is I'm supposed to be appraising. At the moment it's slipped my mind."

Spooner sees an opening and offers himself as a secretary (Foster is young and a poet, and young poets should travel). But Hirst does not hear, and neither Briggs nor Foster seem menaced by this offer. The three friends join together in a drink, the curtains are drawn, the lamps are lit, and these three "oldest of friends" celebrate their relationship. Spooner launches into an impassioned plea for the job (as earnestly seeking it as Davies fails to do)—offering piety, prudence, liberality and goodness, undying loyalty—and even a poetry reading for Hirst at the Bulls Head. But Hirst casually suggests that they change the subject. For the last time. And then he realizes what he had said. Foster and Briggs now have him in their power—the dream of drowning was false; there can be neither life nor death nor change in No Man's Land—and Spooner sadly agrees:

> No. You are in no man's land. Which never moves, which never changes, which never grows older, but which remains forever, icy and silent.

Silence
HIRST: I'll drink to that.
He drinks.
     SLOW FADE

VII   *Critical Responses*

The difficulty with *No Man's Land* is in separating performance from the play. Whatever the quality of the play Richardson and Gielgud made it an evening to remember in the theater. Irving Wardle, in *The Times* (April 25), saw no man's land as "that uncharted territory where dreams, memories and actuality meet on equal terms" and

pointed out that the fruitful partnership between these two knights of
the theater in David Storey's *Home* was continued here; though he
was less happy about the use to which that partnership was put. Trac-
ing echoes of Eliot and Beckett he still concluded that it remained
"palpably the work of our best living playwright in its command of
language and power to erect a coherent structure in a twilight zone of
confusion and dismay" which received a production of burnished pre-
cision in John Bury's set—a sunlit refuge and an inescapable cell: "The
play makes its effects with total confidence: the objection is that effect
has been raised into a first priority." Hobson (*The Sunday Times*, April
27) was full of praise for Pinter, Richardson, Gielgud, and Peter Hall,
but baffled by the play, while B. A. Young (*Financial Times*, April 25)
suggested that the meaning is only what you see and hear and that this
latest statement of familiar Pinter formulae says it beautifully. So we
can agree that Pinter's craftsmanship remains, but what of his instinct?
That, too, remains—illustrated, for example, by the private joke in
naming the characters after four cricketers! Pinter admits choosing
them (as he would not admit choosing them in *Silence*) halfway
through the writing "because they were appropriate." Hirst, Briggs,
and Foster were all-rounders and left-arm bowlers while Spooner was
known for his elegant stroke-play. Both Gale and Esslin have taken this
clue and described the play as a cricket match. The American critic's
description is decidedly that of a foreigner: in cricket matches "everyone stands around in obscure relationships to one another, occasionally
making sudden unexplained movements which are marked off by
pauses and silences."[6] The game is perhaps better described by Esslin
as a game "of subtle positioning and indirect approaches, and a sport
depending on immense staying power and team spirit. Hirst, Foster,
and Briggs are stonewalling against a powerful and subtle attacker."[7]

The *Oxford English Dictionary* defines "no man's land" as "the
name of a plot of ground, lying outside the north wall of London and
used as a place of execution." In the First World War it was the name
given to that area between the trenches which belonged to neither of
the sides fighting but which shifted as one side got the advantage over
the other. *Brewster's Dictionary of Phrase and Fable* adds the information that the name was applied to odd scraps of land, also called
Jack's land, which is interesting since one of the characters is called
Jack. He is also called Foster which allows the implications of foster
son and foster father should we care to pursue them. Gabbard sees the
spaces between the characters as no man's lands; as in *Landscape* and

Silence all the characters are isolated (Spooner is as much a rejecter as rejected); but as the cricket match analogy suggests the spaces are only apparently random—Hirst and his servants, if that is what they are, make up a team or family, whether or not we accept Esslin's suggestion that the basis for that family is a homosexual one. Again a team analogy removes the need to explain in that way.

Clearly the play is full of echoes, memories: *The Servant* (which is master and which servant?); *The Caretaker* (Spooner's hopes of getting a foothold seem to be defeated); *Old Times* (one reminiscence is played off against another); *Tea Party* (the difficulties of success); while Briggs and Foster are a pair strongly recalling *The Dumb Waiter* or *The Birthday Party*, or Lenny and Joey in *The Homecoming* (with Spooner keeping his equilibrium like Teddy?); and, of course, much of the memories about sex and games in country houses, the appearance of innocence and order covering deceit and perversion must have been helped by Pinter's work on *The Go-Between*. The extra pressure brought to bear here must be the passing of time, that is, growing old—when choices are limited and "life congeals into the immutable winter of the no man's land between life and death."[8] Spooner is not excluded at the end—which is as open as that of *The Caretaker;* indeed the characters may all be frozen like a photograph; or like the characters in *Huis Clos*.

Noticeably, too, there is an increased use of certain four-letter words in this play, which is surprising. *Landscape* had, of course, been banned for such words and clearly Pinter has a new freedom since the end of censorship—though he himself wishes to use it sparingly:

I object to one thing to do with sex: this scheme afoot on the part of many "liberal-minded" persons to open up the obscene language to general commerce. It should be the dark secret language of the underworld. There are very few words—you shouldn't kill them by overuse. I have used such words once or twice in my plays, but I couldn't get them through the Lord Chamberlain. They're great, wonderful words, but must be used very sparingly. The pure publicity of freedom of language fatigues me, because it's a demonstration rather than something said.[9]

Such words are used less sparingly in *No Man's Land* than anywhere else; but they are still used strategically. Obviously there is a strong comedy element in the sudden descent from high-flown talk to the blunt brevity of the barrack-room—and both are meaningless! But the descent also makes a point. If Spooner threatens the relationship in the house, and the family, he does so because he can talk like Hirst, match memory with memory. Briggs and Foster cut this flow short. It is difficult to match obscenity or to modulate upon it fruitfully. And in the end the flow of words traps the characters. It is Foster who recognizes the words that trap Hirst philosophically and semantically— when he expresses a wish to change things he in fact ensures that there can be no change. "As it is" are the first words of the play. Wealth has brought security, even luxury, but old age has brought on impotence and the need for society, friends, a family, grows more urgent. The play, surely, contrasts the companionship offered by Spooner with the security offered by Briggs and Foster; Spooner's assurance of style is exposed by Briggs and Foster whose language hints at violence and their class: "The opposition of the manners of the country and the town in the comedy of the late seventeenth century has given way here, as in *The Homecoming*, to a conflict of the different social classes."[10]

And they are all, of course, interdependent.

The play has been dismissed by some critics: Peter Thomson thinks it is, perhaps, an "elaborate spoof"[11] but gives no real evidence for this feeling. Even Michael Coveney, in *Plays and Players* (July 1975), was lukewarm, suggesting that Pinter was writing, perhaps, about alcoholism. His frequent use of "perhaps" suggests a failure of nerve; and anyway alcoholism is a symptom surely, not the thing itself? Coveney feels that Briggs and Foster (he gets the names wrong and writes Hirst and Briggs!) are not geared to the development of a theatrical statement and only presented "lazily" in anecdotal form; but he concludes: "If Pinter's dramatic scheme for once has gone awry, the prose is as masterly as ever. And when spoken as it is here, by what must surely be the funniest double-act in town, I would only willingly compare it with that of Congreve or Shaw."

CHAPTER 9

Close of Play

*B*ETRAYAL opened at the National Theatre on November 15, 1978, and if Pinter has often been accused of being enigmatic in this play he had his revenge: we know more or less everything and the knowing does us no good. It is a play in nine scenes covering the years 1968–77, only time runs backward. This is no problem since the program *tells* you it is running backward. It is also, which is unusual for a Pinter stage play, set in seven different locations over nine years involving all the four seasons of the year. This involved the use of a very slow revolve and rather cramped John Bury in his designs. It is, in every way, a cluttered play and more suitable, one would think, for television than for the stage.

The characters are all from a particular class: a publisher, a literary agent, an art gallery owner, and a doctor—although only three of these characters appear: Jerry, his best friend, Robert, and Robert's wife, Emma. Jerry's wife appears to be always on duty off-stage and the children are also kept off-stage. The story (and there obviously is one) concerns an affair between Jerry and Emma and the various betrayals that surround that affair. In Scene 1, 1977, Jerry and Emma meet in a pub. It is spring and their affair has been over for some time (indeed Emma seems to be having an affair now with an author called Casey) and Jerry is uneasy about the meeting. He is even more disturbed when Emma tells him that she had a long talk with Robert the previous night to discuss the end of the marriage and discovered that Robert had been betraying her by having affairs. She then told Robert about her affair with Jerry. Jerry is so upset that he phones Robert, later, who tells him that he has known about the affair for four years. This upsets Jerry as much as the fact that he did not know that Robert had been having affairs; as his best friend he feels he should have guessed. But as Robert says: he didn't know much about anything, really.

Scene 3 takes place in the flat which Jerry and Emma took for their affair; now, in 1975 the affair is ending, the afternoons are over. Scene

4 is set in the living room of Robert and Emma's house and shows the three friends together discussing work and the game of squash, which is a male preserve. In Scene 5 Robert and Emma are in Venice and Robert discovers (in 1973) that Emma and Jerry have been betraying him for five years. Emma assures him that Ned is his child since Jerry was away for two months in America and so could not be the father. The next scene shows Emma just back from Venice, in the flat with Jerry. Jerry is worried in case his wife should have discovered their relationship through a letter; Emma does not tell him that Robert has discovered it—through a letter. Nor does Robert tell him in the next scene when he has lunch with Jerry, though Robert is aggressively drunk. However, Robert does say that he went to Torcello, whereas Emma had told Jerry they had not. And the offer to play squash is still open.

Scene 8 is in 1971, showing the lovers, Emma and Jerry, taking the flat for their affair; Emma tells Jerry she is pregnant but the child is Robert's. And the final scene shows the beginning of the affair at a party at Robert and Emma's house when Jerry, Robert's best friend and best man, becomes Emma's best man.

I *Critical Responses*

The play's reception was lukewarm—rather like my summary above! Michael Billington, in the *Guardian* (November 16, 1978), admitted that the play was full of technical resource but was distressed by "the pitifully thin strip of human experience it explores and its obsession with the tiny ripples on the stagnant pond of bourgeois-affluent life." The title announces the theme but amongst the betrayals the play shows is Pinter's own—of his immense talent—"by serving up this kind of high-class soap-opera (laced with suitable cultural brand-names like Venice, Torcello, and Yeats) instead of a real play." The play's technical finesse may make interesting discussion at drama faculty level but it offers little pleasure for the playgoer. John Barber, in the *Daily Telegraph* (November 16), felt that he had not seen a play but "an intricate and unimportant machine," though the subject, deceit, could have been impressive: "Deceit, the leprous distilment brewed by the conniving trio, creeps through their veins and curdles their intercourse, sexual and social, until it poisons everything that was healthy and natural between them. But it was like watching specimens under glass. . . ." Milton Shulman, in the *Evening Standard* (November 16), commented that many women's magazines would be prepared to print it without changing a line and quoted the obvious reference to the title from Scene 5 where Robert and Emma are discussing Spink's new book which Robert has rejected. Emma wants to know why:

ROBERT: Oh . . . not much more to say on that subject, really, is there?
EMMA: What do you consider the subject to be?
ROBERT: Betrayal.
EMMA: No, it isn't.

This might be a clue? B. A. Young found no complexities in the straightforward tale of multiple adultery which puts forward the rival claims of wife and mistress (a familiar theme): "What makes it such a dull one in this instance is that Mr. Pinter has made his characters such uninteresting people." He concedes that Pinter may have intended this, but even the story is uninteresting because "there is the threat hanging over us all the time that we know precisely how the play must end." Unfortunately few critics pursued this matter of the ending, which is, of course, the beginning. Bernard Levin, in *The Sunday Times* (November 19), who has always felt that the devices covered "a desperate poverty of thought and feeling," even in a play like *The Caretaker*, now finds that Pinter gives this away and rather hankers for the old-fashioned acrostics: "There is no sign of any interest, on the part of Mr. Pinter, in these people, their lives or their feelings; not surprisingly, they therefore arouse no interest of their own." This was a view echoed by Robert Cushman in *The Observer* (November 19):

We learn a lot about the world of the three characters, and Mr. Pinter is as adept as ever in slipping immensely suggestive detail on to a bland canvas. These details, however, are merely sociological; we learn almost nothing about the characters as individuals and thus—since their situation is hardly original—can take no very lively interest in them.
    In fact this play, apparently so free with its revelations, comes over as its author's most tightlipped. (There are, untypically, no set-piece speeches). It is a good joke, though whether on us or him I am unsure. The title, though, begins to resonate. Obviously Emma and Jerry betray Robert, and Robert betrays Emma with an affair of his own, and betrays Jerry by not admitting the extent of his knowledge, and there is an off-stage character called Casey, a successful writer who inherits Emma and may be the arch-traitor. But the structure of the play is literally a betrayal and figuratively as well since it is

treasonous to what have been assumed, perhaps too glibly, to be Mr. Pinter's dramatic principles.

It was left to Martin Esslin to ask the obvious question, in *Plays and Players* (January 1979): Is this a new Pinter? Pointing out that the play tells a realistic story of adultery in London middle-class intellectual circles, spelled out in convincing detail so that the only unusual thing is that the story is told backwards, he feels that there is "much more in the play than meets the first casually observing glance. It is—like so many earlier Pinter—far more subtle than first impressions might suggest." Of course he may simply be reluctant to point out that the emperor has no clothes. But he sees the reversal of the scenes as a new variation on the fallibility of memory: the sting lies in the beginning—that the affair we witness started "almost casually, out of drunkenness," and the husband taking it as no more than politeness withdraws and leaves them together. The central point of the play is that the emotion between these characters, their relationship "on a personal, intellectual, spiritual plane, is shown as totally arid, in fact, non-existent. That, to my mind is the point the play is making. And it is by no means a trivial point. It is central to the sickness of our society." But as many critics objected the point was that these people never came alive and that their relationship to any society was vestigial. Nor am I quite so convinced that Robert is so blind or simple-minded as Esslin suggests in his review. As played by Daniel Massey Robert suggested depths occasionally that went unanswered in the play. The deadness of the characters has been too successful; this is truly a no man's land and silence without the alluring advantages of a lively language. The banal remains banal. The play has a lightness that should, perhaps, have called forth more comedy—Robert occasionally shows flashes of wit and irony which suggest why he is so complacent; but his detachment also recalls Teddy in *The Homecoming*, another husband who seemed not to take care of his wife. Here Emma hardly seems worth taking care of. Indeed Robert's wit moves him into a detached position which contrasts with Jerry's grubby little apprehensions—about being found out, or having to leave his wife and children. Jerry has, it would seem, a perfect marriage—he rarely sees his wife. Possibly time will tell us more about this play, which is clearly transitional, marking time—and new undercurrents may appear in retrospect. It is tempting to infer something from Pinter's private life which the National Theatre program rather insists on thrusting on us by telling us that Pinter now lives with Antonia Fraser, but neither that nor anything else can alter the impression that here Pinter is only a conjuror, not a magician. The play is dedicated to Simon Gray, whose work Pinter directs and clearly admires and which, here, he seems to have too faithfully imitated.

II Conclusion

So we may be teased by the latest play but not haunted; or perhaps we object merely to the quality of the ghosts? In his acceptance speech at Hamburg in 1970 Pinter described his relationship with his truculent characters: "But there's no question that quite a conflict takes place between the writer and his characters and on the whole I would say the characters are the winners. And that's as it should be, I think. Where a writer sets out a blueprint for his characters, and keeps them rigidly to, where they do not at any time upset his applecart, where he has mastered them, he has also killed them, or rather terminated their birth, and he has a dead play on his hands." To borrow Ronald Hayman's words the explorer has always slowed his pace to that of the entertainer. Pinter has to balance instinct with craft—he is a traditional playwright in his insistence on curtain lines and in looking for an overall shape or unity—the visual with the verbal, or as Esslin puts it a combination of extreme naturalism of surface description and dreamlike poetic feeling.

It is precisely the instinctual quality in his work that refutes Trussler's easy judgment that Pinter is not interested in what his work is about—when Pinter says that good writing excites him and makes life worth living the verb is precise: excites. What seems to haunt Pinter recently is growing old, deadness, partial oblivion—and the obligation to express these themes as positively as possible. If he recalls Beckett he also reminds us of Coward; as Taylor observes:

Harold Pinter, most intelligent of British dramatists, is just about the least intellectual. That is to say, all his conscious exercise of intelligence goes into the shaping of material which is somehow given . . . rather than in the elaboration of the material itself, or a cool inquiry into its sources and significance. Instinct clearly plays an enormous part in his work. . . . [1]

Such instinct may lose its nerve but never, surely, die. Which is why Pinter will survive. Of all contemporary British dramatists he alone manages to be topical, local, and universal—to give a shape to unconscious impulses and record ordinary behavior. Of his own work he has said, modestly: "I am very concerned with the shape and consistency of mood of my plays. I cannot write anything that appears to me to be loose and unfinished. I like a feeling of order in what I write."[2] His success rests on that sense of order; he is, among his contemporaries, precisely, the *miglior fabbro*.

Notes and References

Chapter One

1. "Poetry and Drama," *On Poetry and Poets* (London, 1957), p. 82.
2. The verse drama of Christopher Fry never presented such a challenge; its weakness was a strong tendency to use verse merely to decorate a romantic action rather than to create a new dramatic form. Fry has been more successful in producing verse drama than his avowed master T. S. Eliot, but only because Fry avoided certain problems, the most crucial of which was to discuss serious problems and not simply make an audience laugh at a romantic situation deliberately kept unreal. *Curtmantle* (1961) shows Fry discussing ideas, and arguing and the verse is very flat indeed. Eliot's lucid style and sensibility drained his characters of vitality, and Fry has been no more successful. He did, however, create an audience not unfavorable to poetic drama. Something more than what his plays offered was needed; the fantastic existence ornamented with verse yielded no poetic vision of life here and now.
3. John Mander, *The Writer and Commitment* (London, 1961), pp. 22, 180–81.
4. George E. Wellwarth, *The Theater of Protest and Paradox* (New York, 1964), pp. 225, 243.
5. "Dans Les Armes de la Ville," *Cahiers de la Compagnie Madeleine Renaud Jean-Louis Barrault*, Paris, No. 20 (October 1957), quoted Martin Esslin, *The Theater of the Absurd* (New York, 1961), p. xix.
6. Quoted in David Tutaev, "The Theater of the Absurd—How Absurd?" *Gambit* 2 (n.d.), 70.
7. *The Sunday Times* (March 4, 1962).
8. Lloyd Alexander (trans.), Jean-Paul Sartre's *Nausea* (London, 1962), p. 173.
9. Iris Murdoch, *Sartre* (London, 1961), p. 13.
10. F. N. Lees, "Samuel Beckett," *Manchester Memoirs* CIV: 4 (1961–1962).
11. Tynan, *Tynan on Theater*, p. 63.
12. See Robert Brustein, *The Theater of Revolt* (London, 1965), Chapter VII.
13. See D. Krause, *Sean O'Casey, The Man and His Work* (London, 1960), Chapter 2, where the bastard genre is discussed as one of the forms of twentieth-century drama. Dramatists as varied as Shakespeare, Chekhov,

161

Shaw, Synge, O'Casey, Pirandello, Giraudoux, Anouilh, Sartre, Wilder, Beckett, and Ionesco are all shown to have used music-hall devices!

14. Maurice Charney, *Comedy High and Low* (London, 1978), p. 112.

15. Martin Esslin, *Pinter: A Study of His Plays* (London, 1977), p. 236.

16. Lois G. Gordon, *Stratagems to Uncover Nakedness* (Columbia, Missouri, 1969), p. 8.

17. Lucine P. Gabbard, *The Dream Structure of Pinter's Plays: A Psychoanalytic Approach* (1976), p. 36.

18. William Baker and Stephen E. Tabachnik, *Harold Pinter* (Edinburgh, New York, 1973), p. 7.

19. Katherine H. Burkman, *The Dramatic World of Harold Pinter—Its Basis in Ritual* (Columbus, Ohio, 1971), p. 10.

20. "Writing for Myself," *Twentieth Century* CLXIX: 1008 (February, 1961), 172–75. Mr. Pinter regards this article as unsatisfactory; it was compiled by Findlater from the tape of an interview.

Chapter Two

1. Quoted Baker/Tabachnik, p. 3.

2. Ibid., p. 17.

3. Interview with Lawrence M. Bensky for the *Paris Review*, reprinted in *Pinter: A Collection of Critical Essays*, edited by Arthur Ganz (Englewood Cliffs, N.J., 1972), p. 29.

4. "Harold Pinter Replies," *New Theater Magazine* XI: 2 (January 1961), 8–10.

5. Quoted in Esslin, *Pinter*, p. 34.

6. Interview, the *New Yorker*, February 25, 1967.

7. Speech to Student Drama Festival, *The Sunday Times*, March 4, 1962.

8. Dirk Bogarde, *Snakes and Ladders* (London, 1978), p. 235.

9. Speech to Student Drama Festival.

10. Quoted in John Russell Brown, *Theatre Language* (London, 1972), p. 27.

11. August Strindberg, *Plays*, translated by Michael Meyer (London, 1964), pp. 98–99.

12. Austin E. Quigley, *The Pinter Problem* (Princeton, N.J., 1975), p. 29.

13. Andrew Kennedy, *Six Dramatists in Search of a Language* (Cambridge, 1975), p. 173.

14. See "Pinter Translated," *Encounter* (March 1968), 45–47.

15. Katharine J. Worth, *Revolutions in Modern English Drama* (London, 1972), p. 98.

16. Interview with Bensky, Ganz, p. 22.

17. Ronald Hayman, *Theatre and Anti-Theatre* (London, 1979), p. 125.

Chapter Three

1. Sykes, p. 27.
2. Esslin, p. 43.
3. The *Observer* profile (September 15, 1963) attributed the name "da Pinta" to Pinter's Portuguese ancestry. But Pinter himself, in a letter to me dated April 28, 1964, pointed out that this was very remote.
4. Baker/Tabachnik, p. 18.
5. "Harold Pinter Replies."
6. *The Room* (New York, 1961), p. 99.
7. Ibid., p. 110.
8. Ibid., p. 118.
9. Quoted in Esslin, p. 21.
10. Ibid., p. 66.
11. Clifford Leech, "Two Romantics: Arnold Wesker and Harold Pinter," in Brown and Harris, *Contemporary Theater*, p. 26.
12. John Russell Taylor, *Anger and After*, p. 287.
13. Bensky, reprinted Ganz, p. 20.
14. *The Birthday Party* (New York, 1961), p. 32.
15. Cf. the gloss of this device in Jack Kerouac, *The Town and the City* (New York, 1950), pp. 375 ff.
16. *The Birthday Party*, p. 54.
17. Ibid., p. 59.
18. Ibid., p. 80.
19. Ibid., p. 84.
20. Pinter has since changed this to less formal wear.
21. Irving Wardle, *Encore* (July-August 1958), 39-40.
22. Bert O. States, *Irony and Drama* (Ithaca, N. Y., and London, 1971), p. 127.
23. Bernard Dukore, "The Theater of Harold Pinter," *Tulane Drama Review* VI: 3 (March 1962), 55-68.
24. Quigley, p. 66.
25. *The Birthday Party*, p. 88.
26. R. F. Storch, in Ganz, pp. 138-39.
27. Gregorz Sinko, "Stara i Mtoda Anglia," *Dialog* LX: 4 (April 1961), 97-99.
28. Simon Trussler, *The Plays of Harold Pinter* (London, 1973), p. 46.
29. Baker/Tabachnik, pp. 57-58.
30. Taylor, *Anger and After*, p. 290.
31. *The Dumb Waiter* (New York, 1961), pp. 102-103.
32. Steven H. Gale, *butter's going up: a critical analysis of Harold Pinter's work* (Durham, N.C., 1977), p. 59.

33. Tom Maschler (ed.) *New English Dramatists*, No. 3, Introduction by J. W. Lambert (Harmondsworth, Middlesex, 1961) pp. 9–10.
34. *A Slight Ache* (New York, 1962), p. 35.
35. Trussler, p. 64.
36. See Chapter 6 for discussion of "Tea Party."
37. Bensky, reprinted Ganz, p. 29.
38. *A Slight Ache and Other Plays* (London, 1961), p. 121.
39. Recorded by Kenneth Williams. See bibliography.
40. Quoted in Taylor, *Anger and After*, p. 296.
41. *A Slight Ache and Other Plays*, p. 47.
42. Ibid., p. 87.
43. Burkman, p. 97.
44. Taylor, *Anger and After*, p. 307.
45. Wellwarth, *The Theater of Protest and Paradox*, p. 208.
46. "Writing for Myself."
47. Ibid.
48. Cf. the following extract from Sartre's *Nausea*, p. 169.

I murmur: "It's a seat," a little like an exorcism. But the word stays on my lips: it refuses to go and put itself on the things. It stays what it is, with its red plush, thousands of little red paws in the air; all still, little dead paws, this belly floating in this car, in this grey sky, is not a seat. It could just as well be a dead donkey tossed about in the water, floating with the current, belly in the air in a great grey river, a river of floods; and I could be sitting on the donkey's belly, my feet dangling in the clear water. Things are divorced from their names. They are there, grotesque, headstrong, gigantic and it seems ridiculous to call them seats or say anything at all about them: I am in the midst of things, nameless things. Alone, without words, defenceless, they surround me, are beneath me, behind me, above me. They demand nothing, they don't impose themselves: they are there.

49. Wellwarth, *The Theater of Protest and Paradox*, p. 208.
50. Phrases like "butter's up" and "gentleman's gentleman" recur in *The Servant*. It is surely the poet in Pinter that savors these phrases.
51. *The Dwarfs* (New York, 1962), p. 91.
52. Ibid., pp. 99–100, 101.
53. Ibid., pp. 103–104.
54. Ibid., p. 108.
55. BBC Transcript, *New Comment* (this accounts for the oddness of punctuation and the erratic grammar of the passages quoted).
56. Murdoch, *Sartre*, p. 35.
57. Taylor, *Anger and After*, pp. 307–308.
58. Gabbard, p. 140.
59. Baker/Tabachnik, p. 44.

60. Storch, in Ganz, p. 144.

61. Esslin, p. 119.

Chapter Four

1. Bensky, reprinted Ganz, p. 28.

2. Esslin, p. 102.

3. Leech, "Two Romantics: Arnold Wesker and Harold Pinter," p. 14.

4. Kitchin, "Backwards and Forwards," *Twentieth Century* CLXIX: 1008 (February 1961), 168–69.

5. "Writing for Myself."

6. Esslin, pp. 105, 109, 110.

7. Gabbard, p. 106.

8. Bensky, reprinted Ganz, p. 28.

9. Tynan interview, Esslin, *The Theater of the Absurd*, p. 212.

10. *The Caretaker* (New York, 1961), p. 34.

11. Ibid., p. 46.

12. Ibid., p. 60.

13. Ibid., pp. 63–64.

14. Ibid., p. 70.

15. Ibid., p. 76.

16. Ibid., p. 77.

17. The film more or less followed the Samuel French Acting Edition at this point, inserting dialogue:

MICK *and* ASTON *look at each other then both smile faintly.*
MICK tentatively indicates the pieces of the broken Buddha.
MICK: Look I. . . .
(ASTON regards the pieces then looks at MICK.) Look, what about . . .
(MICK *breaks off, goes to door and exits, leaving it open.*)

The great difficulty in the theater is to convey that smile.

18. Baker/Tabachnik, p. 78.

19. Trussler, p. 85.

20. Donner took Bates into his next film, *Nothing But the Best*, the story of the rise to fame and wealth of a smooth-tongued Cockney boy whose ambitions and methods are ruthless.

21. "Filming 'The Caretaker,'" *Transatlantic Review* 13 (Summer 1963), 17–26.

22. BBC Transcript, *New Comment* (see note 55, Chapter 3).

23. John Russell Taylor, *Sight and Sound* (Winter 1963), 38–39.

24. Taylor, *Anger and After*, pp. 299–302.

25. John Arden, *New Theater Magazine* 1: 4 (July 1960), 29–30.

Chapter Five

1. "Writing for Myself."
2. "Harold Pinter Replies."
3. James's surname is "Horne," which has implications of cuckoldry.
4. *The Collection* (New York, 1962), pp. 77–78.
5. This, like the crucial smile in *The Caretaker*, is a difficult image to capture outside television.
6. John Russell Taylor, *Plays and Players* (August 1962), p. 20.
7. *The Lover* (London, 1963), p. 57.
8. Ibid., p. 71.
9. Ibid., p. 74.
10. Ibid., p. 83.
11. Trussler, p. 114.
12. Anthony Storr, *Sexual Deviations* (Harmondsworth, Middlesex, 1964), p. 40.
13. Taylor, *Anger and After*, pp. 311–12.
14. Esslin, p. 136.

Chapter Six

1. See Gabbard, p. 176.
2. Bensky, reprinted Ganz, p. 22.
3. Esslin, p. 168.
4. Baker/Tabachnik, p. 51.
5. Gabbard, pp. 169–70.
6. Trussler, p. 118.
7. Bensky, reprinted Ganz, p. 26.
8. Gale, p. 38.
9. Baker/Tabachnik, pp. 123–24.
10. "Pinter in Print," *Jewish Quarterly* (Autumn 1968).
11. *The Homecoming* (London, 1965), p. 62.
12. Esslin, p. 149.
13. *The Homecoming*, p. 20.
14. Ibid., p. 40.
15. Ibid., p. 9.
16. Ibid., p. 37.
17. Ibid., p. 42.
18. Ibid., p. 46.
19. The speech was altered in production. The original script read:

Because we know something about the values which have been handed down to us. We may be a little dull, but we still have an eye for mother nature, and often in fact sit out in the back yard having a quiet gander at the night sky. Our little community, our quiet little group, our team, you might say, our unit, made up of, I'll admit it, various and not entirely similar component parts, but which, put together, do nevertheless make up a whole. An organism, which, though we're not exactly a sentimental family, we do recognise as such. And you're an integral part of it, Ted. When we all sit out there in the backyard looking up at the night sky, often as not there's an empty chair standing in the circle, which is in fact yours. And so when you at length return to us, we do expect a bit of grace, a bit of je ne sais quoi, a bit of generosity of mind, a bit of liberality of spirit, to reassure us. We do expect that. But do we get it? Have we got it? Is that what you've given us?

20. Ganz, p. 148.
21. Esslin, pp. 154–55.
22. John Russell Brown, p. 109.
23. Worth, p. 94.
24. *The Homecoming*, p. 29.
25. Quigley, p. 207.
26. Esslin, p. 156.
27. Reported in Gale, p. 146.
28. "Probing Pinter's Play," interview with Henry Hewes, *Saturday Review* (April 8, 1967), 57.

Chapter Seven

1. Harold Pinter talks to Michael Dean, *Listener* (March 6, 1969).
2. Bensky, reprinted Ganz, pp. 23–24.
3. *Plays and Players* (January 1971).
4. Tom Milne, ed., *Losey on Losey*. (London, 1967), p. 21.
5. BBC Transcript, *New Comment* (see note 55, Chapter 3)
6. Losey, p. 135.
7. "Joseph Losey and 'The Servant,'" *Film* 38, (n.d.) p. 28.
8. John Russell Taylor, *Sight and Sound* (Winter 1963/4), pp. 38–39.
9. Penelope Mortimer, *The Pumpkin Eater* (Harmondsworth, Middlesex, 1964), p. 118.
10. Bogarde, *Snakes and Ladders*, p. 246.
11. Losey, p. 14.
12. Baker/Tabachnik, p. 104.
13. James Monaco, *Alain Resnais* (London; New York, 1978), pp. 61–62.
14. Baker/Tabachnik, p. 148.

Chapter Eight

1. John Russell Brown, *Theatre Language*, p. 91.
2. Quoted Esslin, p. 175.

3. John Russell Taylor, *Harold Pinter* (London, 1969), pp. 22–23.

4. See Worth, pp. 48 ff.

5. See John Francis Lane, "No Sex, Please, I'm English," *Plays and Players* (July 1973).

6. Gale, p. 203.

7. Esslin, p. 199.

8. Ibid., p. 200.

9. Bensky, reprinted Ganz, p. 31.

10. David L. Hirst, *Comedy of Manners*, Critical Idiom, No. 40 (London, 1979), p. 80.

11. *Critical Quarterly* 20: 4 (Winter 1978).

Chapter Nine

1. Taylor, *Harold Pinter*, pp. 29–30.

2. "Harold Pinter Replies."

Selected Bibliography

Although Pinter has revised many of his texts I have used the first editions throughout this study.

PRIMARY SOURCES

1. Plays

The Birthday Party and The Room. New York: Grove Press, 1961.

The Caretaker and The Dumb Waiter. New York: Grove Press, 1961.

A recording of the soundtrack of the film of *The Caretaker* is available on Oriole MG 20093–4.

Three Plays: The Collection, A Slight Ache, The Dwarfs. New York: Grove Press, 1962.

The Homecoming. New York: Grove Press, 1966. A recording of the film of *The Homecoming* is available on Caedmon Records, CDL 5361.

The Lover, Tea Party, The Basement. New York: Grove Press, 1967.

A Night Out, Night School, Revue Sketches. New York: Grove Press, 1968.

The Dwarfs and Eight Revue Sketches. New York: Dramatists' Play Service, 1965. Includes: "Trouble in the Works," "The Black and White," "Request Stop," "Last to Go," "Applicant," "Interview," "That's All," and "That's Your Trouble." A recording of "Last to Go" by Kenneth Williams is available on *Pieces of Eight*, Decca SKL 4084, and *Kenneth Williams*, Decca DFE 8548.

Landscape and Silence. New York: Grove Press, 1970. Includes "Night."

Old Times. New York: Grove Press, 1971.

Monologue. London: Covent Garden Press, 1975.

No Man's Land. New York: Grove Press, 1975.

Betrayal. New York: Grove Press, 1979.

The Hothouse. London: Eyre-Methuen Ltd., 1980.

2. Other Writings by Pinter

The poems originally published in *Poetry London* in 1950/51 are now in *Poems*, selected by Alan Clodd. London: Enitharmon Press, 1968.

Poems and Prose, 1949–1977. London: Eyre-Methuen Ltd., 1978. Includes "Kullus," "The Black and White" (prose version), "The Examination," "Tea Party" (story), and "Mac."

Tea Party (story), *Playboy*, January 1965.

"Dialogue for Three," *Stand* (Leeds, 1963–64).

3. Films

Five Screenplays. London: Methuen and Co., Ltd., 1971; New York: Grove Press, 1974. Includes *The Servant, The Pumpkin Eater, The Quiller Memorandum, Accident* and *The Go-Between.*
The Proust Screenplay, London: Eyre-Methuen, Ltd., 1978.

4. Interviews with Pinter

"Harold Pinter Replies," *New Theatre Magazine* XI:2 (January 1961), 8–10.
"Writing For Myself," *Twentieth Century* CLXIX: 1008 (February 1961), 172–75. This issue also contains a poem.
"Harold Pinter and Clive Donner on filming *The Caretaker,*" *Transatlantic Review* 13 (Summer 1963), 17–23.
"Trying to Pin Down Pinter," interview with Marshall Pugh, *Daily Mail* (March 7, 1964).
"Writing for the Theatre," *Evergreen Review* 33 (August–September 1964), 80–82. A reprint of "Between the Lines," Pinter's speech at the Seventh National Students' Drama Festival, Bristol, printed in *The Sunday Times,* March 4, 1962.
"The Art of the Theatre," interview with Laurence M. Bensky, *Paris Review* 39 (Fall 1966), 13–37. Reprinted in *Writers at Work, The Paris Review Interviews, Third Series,* edited by George Plimpton. New York: Viking, 1967.
Interview with John Russell Taylor, *Sight and Sound,* Autumn 1966.
Interview in the *New Yorker,* "Talk of the Town," February 25, 1967.
Interview with Henry Hewes, "Probing Pinter's Plays," *Saturday Review,* April 8, 1967.
Interview with Kathleen Tynan, "In Search of Harold Pinter," *Evening Standard,* Part 1, April 25, 1968; Part 2, April 26, 1968.
Interview with Michael Dean, BBC TV "Late Night Line-up," printed in the *Listener,* March 6, 1969.
The Homecoming: manuscript and notes and a page of the typescript, reproduced in the *London Magazine* 100 (July–August 1969), 153–54.
"Speech: Hamburg 1970," *Theatre Quarterly* I: 3 (July–September 1971).
Interview with Mel Gussow, "A Conversation (Pause) with Harold Pinter," *New York Times Magazine,* December 5, 1971.
Interview with Sidney Edwards, "To Hell and Back with Pinter," *Evening Standard,* May 18, 1979, pp. 28–29.
Interview with John Barber, *Daily Telegraph,* June 23, 1980

SECONDARY SOURCES

1. Bibliographies

GORDON, LOIS G. "Pigeonholing Pinter: A Bibliography." *Theater Documen-*

tation, Fall 1968. This annotated list of books and articles, including some reviews of performances, is still useful but has been overtaken by:

GALE, STEVEN H. *Harold Pinter: an annotated bibliography*. Boston: G. K. Hall and Company, 1979. The most extensive bibliography to date, listing over 2,000 entries.

IMHOF, RUDIGER. *Pinter: A Bibliography*. London and Los Angeles: TQ Publications, Ltd., 1976. Second Full Revised Edition. This is by no means complete; in particular it ignores many American reviews and misses too many reviews of the films.

2. Separate Studies

BAKER, WILLIAM, and TABACHNIK, STEPHEN E. *Harold Pinter*. Edinburgh: Oliver and Boyd, 1973; New York: Barnes and Noble, 1973. Both are lecturers in English at the University of the Negev, Israel, and look at the Jewishness of Pinter up to *Old Times*.

BURKMAN, KATHERINE H. *The Dramatic World of Harold Pinter—Its Basis in Ritual*, Columbus: Ohio State University Press, 1971. Frazer's *The Golden Bough* offers an excellent metaphorical clue to the ritual sacrifices at the center of Pinter's drama.

ESSLIN, MARTIN. *Pinter: A Study of His Plays*. Third Expanded Edition. London: Eyre-Methuen Ltd., 1977. Originally published as *The Peopled Wound*, 1970. Chronology, bibliography (including translations into various languages), and realistic explanations of the plays *and* interpretation of them on the level of dreams up to *No Man's Land*.

GABBARD, LUCINE P. *The Dream Structure of Pinter's Plays: A Psycho-Analytic Approach*. Associated University Presses (Fairleigh Dickinson University Press), 1976. The title is self-explanatory; the works of Sigmund Freud figure largely in the bibliography.

GALE, STEPHEN H. *butter's going up: a critical analysis of Harold Pinter's work*. Durham, N. C.: Duke University Press, 1977. Exhaustive treatment of Pinter's work up to *No Man's Land*. Chronology, lists of awards, acting roles, directing, first performances, cast lists, and a lengthy annotated bibliography. Probably the most complete collection of information to date.

GANZ, ARTHUR (editor). *Pinter: A Collection of Critical Essays*. Englewood Cliffs, N.J.: Prentice-Hall, Inc., 1972. Most of the material is available elsewhere but this collects it, usefully, together.

GORDON, LOIS G. *Stratagems to Uncover Nakedness*. Columbus: University of Missouri Press, 1969. Early Freudian interpretation.

HOLLIS, JAMES R. *Harold Pinter: The Poetics of Silence*. Carbondale: Southern Illinois University Press, 1970.

KERR, WALTER. *Harold Pinter*. New York and London: Columbia University Press, 1967. Not merely the themes in Pinter's plays are existential but they function on existential principles.

LAHR, JOHN (editor). *A Casebook on Harold Pinter's "The Homecoming"*. Interesting collection including interviews with director, designer, and two actors.

QUIGLEY, AUSTIN E. *The Pinter Problem*. Princeton, N.J.: Princeton University Press, 1975. The problem is what new direction can Pinter criticism take after ten years of repeating the same themes and using the same methods. The answer is linguistics, stimulated by Wittgenstein, J. R. Firth, and M. A. K. Halliday. This treatment is applied to *The Room*, *The Caretaker*, *The Homecoming*, and *Landscape*.

SYKES, ALRENE. *Harold Pinter*. St. Lucia: University of Queensland Press, 1970; New York: Humanities Press, 1971.

TAYLOR, JOHN RUSSELL. *Harold Pinter*. London: Longmans Green, 1969.

TRUSSLER, SIMON. *The Plays of Harold Pinter*. London: Victor Gollancz Ltd., 1973. Chronology, cast lists, and a bibliography. Trussler is basically unsympathetic to Pinter; so much so that one cannot see why he bothered to write the book.

3. Books on which Pinter Based His Screenplays and Films

FITZGERALD, F. SCOTT. *The Last Tycoon*. New York: Scribner's, 1941.

FOWLES, JOHN. *The French Lieutenant's Woman*. London: Jonathan Cape, 1969; Boston: Little, Brown and Co., Inc., 1970.

GRAY, SIMON. *Butley*. New York: Viking Press, 1971. Recorded Caedmon Records, TRS 362.

HALL, ADAM. *The Berlin Memorandum*. London: Collins, 1965.

HARTLEY, L. P. *The Go-Between*. London: Hamish Hamilton, 1953; New York: Avon, 1968.

HIGGINS, AIDAN. *Langrishe, Go Down*. London: Calder, 1966; New York: Grove Press, 1966.

MAUGHAM, ROBIN. *The Servant*. London: The Falcon Press, 1948; reprinted Heinemann, 1964; New York; Harcourt Brace, 1949.

MORTIMER, PENELOPE. *The Pumpkin Eater*. London: Hutchinson, 1962.

MOSLEY, NICHOLAS. *Accident*. London: Hodder and Stoughton, 1965.

PROUST, MARCEL. *A La Recherche du Temps Perdu*. Paris: Gallimard, 1919–1927. The standard Pléiade edition is in three volumes.

4. Other Works

BROWN, J. R. *Theatre Language*. London: Allen Lane (Penguin Press), 1972. Language in the theater is not just words. Three chapters (out of seven) are devoted to Pinter.

ESSLIN, MARTIN. *The Theater of the Absurd*. New York: Doubleday and Co., 1961. Claimed Pinter as an absurdist.

EVANS, GARETH LLOYD. *The Language of Modern Drama*. London: Dent, 1977.

HIRST, DAVID L. *Comedy of Manners.* "The Critical Idiom." London: Methuen and Co., Ltd., 1979, pp. 67–81.

KENNEDY, ANDREW. *Six Dramatists in Search of a Language.* Cambridge: Cambridge University Press, 1975. Chapter 4 discusses Pinter.

MANDER, JOHN. *The Writer and Commitment.* London: Secker and Warburg, 1961. Discusses the difficulties of defining "commitment."

MILNE, TOM (editor). *Losey on Losey.* London: Secker and Warburg, 1967.

MONACO, JAMES. *Alain Resnais.* London: Secker and Warburg; New York: Oxford University Press, 1978.

STYAN, J. L. *The Dark Comedy.* Cambridge: Cambridge University Press, 1962. As the title implies, traces the history of the mixed play.

TAYLOR, JOHN RUSSELL. *Anger and After.* London: Methuen and Co., Ltd., 1962, revised 1963; published in America as *The Angry Theater.* New York: Hill and Wang, revised 1962. Useful survey of British theater after 1956.

WORTH, KATHERINE J. *Revolutions in Modern English Drama.* London: G. Bell and Sons, 1972. "Revolutions" here means the turns of a wheel bringing up the past in new forms. Chapter 3 (Joyce via Pinter) and Chapter 6 are useful.

5. Articles

ADLER, THOMAS P. "Pinter's *Night:* A Stroll Down Memory Lane," *Modern Drama* XVII: 4 (December 1974), 461–65.

AMEND, VICTOR E. "Harold Pinter: Some Credits and Debits," *Modern Drama* 10 (September 1967), 165–74.

AYLWIN, TONY. "The Memory of All That: Pinter's *Old Times,*" *English* XXII (1973) 99–102.

BERNHARD, F. J. "Beyond Realism: The Plays of Harold Pinter," *Modern Drama* III: 2 (September 1965), 185–91. Discusses symbols and rhythms in dialogue that although apparently realistic and dealing with realistic situations becomes something more than realism.

BROWN, JOHN RUSSELL. "Mr. Pinter's Shakespeare," *Critical Quarterly* V: 3 (Autumn 1963), 251–65. Uses Pinter's method—the absence of exposition, development, and conclusion in the formal sense—to look at Shakespeare. Illuminates both Pinter and Shakespeare (with a look at Beckett and Ionesco en route).

———."Dialogue in Pinter and Others," *Critical Quarterly* VII: 3 (Autumn 1965), 225–43. Taking the point of view suggested above Brown examines the dialogue in Pinter's plays as an example of Stanislavsky's "subtext."

CUSHMAN, ROBERT. "Mr. Pinter's Spoonerisms," *Observer Review* April 27, 1975, p. 32. Review of *No Man's Land* which compares Spooner to Davies in *The Caretaker.*

DICK, KAY. "Mr. Pinter and the Fearful Matter," *Texas Quarterly* IV: 3 (Autumn 1961), 257–65. Reads the plays as a sequence in which violence is gradually eliminated and passive resistance triumphs (in *The Caretaker*). Makes a useful distinction between Davies and the "tramps" of Samuel Beckett.

DUKORE, BERNARD. "The Theater of Harold Pinter," *Tulane Drama Review* VI: 3 (March 1962), 43–54. Pinter's plays reflect the tensions and attitudes of present-day England, no longer a colonial power, and show man being reduced to a cipher.

EIGO, JAMES. "Pinter's *Landscape*," *Modern Drama* 16 (September 1973), 179–83.

ESSLIN, MARTIN. "Pinter Translated: On International Non-Communication," *Encounter* XXX: 3 (March 1968), 45–47. And in Martin Esslin, *Brief Chronicles* (1970), 190–95.

GOLDSTONE, HERBERT. "Not So Puzzling Pinter: *The Homecoming*," *Theatre Annual* 25 (1969), 20–27. Male and female attitudes to sex are contrasted in *The Homecoming*.

HOEFER, JACQUELINE. "Pinter and Whiting: Two Attitudes towards the Alienated Artist," *Modern Drama* IV (February 1962), 402–408. Interesting comparison between two plays about a birthday (*Saint's Day* and *The Birthday Party*) both of which treat the artist as an outsider.

KAUFMAN, M. W. "Actions That a Man Might Play: Pinter's *The Birthday Party*," *Modern Drama* 16 (September 1973), 167–78.

KNIGHT, WILSON. "The Kitchen Sink," *Encounter* XXI: 6 (December 1963), 48–54. Examines the contrast between dynamic outsider and civilized man in contemporary drama. His interpretation of *The Caretaker* is not supported by the text.

MARCUS, FRANK. "Pinter: The Pause that Refreshes," *New York Times*, July 12, 1969. Review of *Landscape* and *Silence* which discusses the use of language and particularly pauses and silences.

MARTINEAU, STEPHEN. "Pinter's *Old Times*: the Memory Game," *Modern Drama* XVI: 3–4 (December 1973) 287–97.

MORRIS, KELLY. "The Homecoming," *Tulane Drama Review* XI: 2 (Winter 1966), 185–91. An analysis of *The Homecoming* as a type of modern comedy of manners showing aggressive dialogue within a format of excessive decorum; the theme is restoration, through Ruth, of a matriarchy.

NELSON, HUGH. "*The Homecoming*: Kith and Kin." In John Russell Brown, *Modern British Dramatists*, pp. 145–63.

SCHECHNER, RICHARD. "Puzzling Pinter," *Tulane Drama Review* XI: 2 (Winter 1966), 176–84. Discusses the "incompleteness" of Pinter's plays, suggesting that, as a disinterested artist, Pinter is asking: What can theater do? The realistic attention of an audience focused on an illusionistic presentation leads to an insoluble riddle.

SINKO, GREGORZ. "Stara i Mtoda Anglia," *Dialogue* LX: 4 (April 1961), 97–99. Discusses three early plays in the tradition of Franz Kafka.

THOMSON, PETER. "Harold Pinter: a retrospect," *Critical Quarterly* 20: 4 (Winter 1978), 21–28. Feels that Pinter has lost confidence as a dramatist and let his admirers down. This is not an uncommon view.

WALKER, AUGUSTA. "Messages from Pinter," *Modern Drama* 10: 1 (May 1967), 1–10. Pinter's plays are allegories of life but also concerned with what drives people in their relationships with others.

Index

176